LEARN TO
DISCERN

LEARN TO DISCERN

ROBERT G. DEMOSS, JR.
FOREWORD BY JOSH MCDOWELL

ZondervanPublishingHouse
Grand Rapids, Michigan

A Division of HarperCollinsPublishers

Learn to Discern
© 1992 by Robert G. DeMoss, Jr.

Requests for information should be addressed to:
Zondervan Publishing House
Grand Rapids, Michigan 49530

DeMoss, Robert G.
    Learn to discern / Robert G. DeMoss, Jr. – 1st ed.
      p.   cm.
    Includes bibliographical references (p.   ) and index.
    ISBN 0-310-51831-8 (pbk.)
    1. United States—Popular culture. 2. Mass media—Social aspects—
United States. I. Title.
E169.12.D39   1992
302.23'4'0973–dc20   91–44310
                                             CIP

Unless otherwise noted, all Scripture quotations are from the New American Standard Bible, © 1960, 1962, 1963, 1968, 1971, 1972, 1973, 1975, 1977, by The Lockman Foundation and are used by permission.

Cover design by Steve Diggs & Friends, Nashville, Tennessee

Printed in the United States of America

92 92 94 95 96 97 98 / LB / 10 9 8 7 6 5 4 3 2

This book is dedicated to
my wonderful mother and father:

Your love, prayers, and
godly example are the primary
reasons these pages exist today.
I pray that one day I will be able
to continue the legacy that you've
fostered through a family of my own.

I love you
more than words can say.

CONTENTS

FOREWORD

*L*et me ask you a question. What percentage of Christian young people would you estimate are engaged in pre-marital sexual activity during their high school years? 10 percent? 25 percent? As hard as it may be to believe, according to a teen sex survey in eight evangelical denominations, more than 40 percent of churched youth by age eighteen have experienced sexual intercourse. (This revealing study was commissioned by my office in 1987 with the assistance of the Barna Research Group of Glendale, California.)

Over the last decade, I have spent a significant amount of time studying trends in teen sexual behavior. What I discovered shocked me: the pre-marital sexual behavior of Christian young people was virtually identical to those outside of the church. Contrary to what I had assumed, Christian young people were as sexually active as their unsaved friends. This discovery prompted me to launch the "Why Wait?" campaign.

During the last few years, I have spoken to tens of thousands of high school students, challenging them to abstain from sex until marriage. Through my direct involvement with numerous teenagers around the country, and based upon the letters I have received from them, I have come to this conclusion: the decision by a high school student to experiment with sex before marriage is a decision whose roots can be traced to his or her early years of personal development.

In other words, there are a number of outside influences that contribute to a Christian teenagers decision to engage in sex—influences that set the stage from a very young age. Peer pressure is certainly a significant factor. The lack of good communication between youth and their parents certainly is another component of the problem. However, I believe one of the most overlooked and underestimated influences upon teenagers is the role of the popular entertainment culture. Over an extended period of time, the negative ideas found in entertainment can work as a tool that dismantles God-given inhibitions to inappropriate sexual expression.

As Bob DeMoss points out in this eye-opening work, it is time you and I re-acquainted ourselves with the messages that our children receive from advertising, television, film, and music industries—messages that are frequently hostile to the biblical principles we work so hard to instill in our kids. Frankly, it is often not a pretty picture. In fact, you may be offended by some of the evidence that Bob submits for our scrutiny. While this inspection can be taxing, it is an important first step towards understanding the influences that shape the way our young people view their world.

I appreciate the fact that *Learn to Discern* moves beyond this disturbing analysis to a significant study of what we can do to help our families think critically and biblically about entertainment. Bob provides us with practical, biblically-based tools to counteract the negative values which the media parades before the watchful eyes of our children. His emphasis on setting a standard in the home, spending time "nose to nose" affirming the self-esteem of each child, and the many creative ideas he details, makes this book a valuable asset for every parent who desires to prepare their children for a healthy adulthood.

As more adults study *Learn to Discern* and apply the principles contained therein, I believe fewer teenagers would be engaged in sexual promiscuity, acts of violence, and other destructive behaviors routinely glorified by the entertainment industry.

JOSH MCDOWELL

ACKNOWLEDGMENTS

*M*y career, if you can call it that, in writing started when I was about nine years of age when I wrote my first novel. Of course, it numbered all of seven handwritten pages (everyone has to start *somewhere*). My mother, who is the eternal encourager, praised me as if I were the next Tom Clancy. Incidental writing projects aside, my first real taste of publishing was in the spring of 1984. My good friends Cathy and Thom Hickling published a monthly Christian newspaper called *Expression*. Beginning with record and film reviews, I ultimately penned a monthly column on youth culture issues for them. Thanks, guys, for giving me the encouragement to express myself through the printed page.

Next to my parents, Reid Carpenter (president of the Pittsburgh Leadership Foundation) did more to sharpen my burden for young people than any other influence. Reid's heart for teens and love for the Lord made a deep impression upon me in the early days of my career as a communicator on youth issues. Thanks, Reid, for providing a faithful example of Christian leadership and for your special insight into a culture that's gone berserk.

Those who have followed my life's work know that I spent five years at the helm of Teen Vision, a nonprofit organization addressing the youth culture, which I founded in Pittsburgh, Pennsylvania. Behind the scenes was the incredible vision and generosity of Gary Ginter that kept Teen Vision properly funded. Because of the sacrificial giving of Gary and his wife Joanna, Teen Vision provided me with a platform to help teenagers evaluate and utilize media and music from a Christian perspective. It was during those five years that many of the principles of this book were nurtured and "field tested."

In similar fashion, I am grateful to the Lord for bringing me to work at Focus on the Family. There, I've had the opportunity to witness firsthand the love, commitment, and dedication of Dr. James Dobson as he seeks to strengthen the family worldwide. Thank you, Dr. Dobson, for allowing me the privilege of working alongside you in this vital task. You have inspired and enabled me to share this message of discernment with families far and wide. And thanks for standing behind me in the wake of my wrestling match with Phil Donahue regarding 2 Live Crew's lyrics.

Many friends challenged me to write this book. Among them are Maru and Pierre Allegre, Chuck Bolte, Sandy Bove, Jennifer Brown, Jim and Jean Daly, Gregg and Gretchen Hansen, Tom Hess, Michael and Karen Jameson, Doug and Cathy Kay, Joanne and Von Letherer, Shelley Reed, Jim and Kim Thomas, Walt and Jane Turner, Stacey Waller, and Tim and Amy Zeffiro. Space doesn't permit me to list all of my co-workers at Focus on the Family who also prayed for this effort. Nonetheless, I thank each of you for pushing me toward the finish line.

I'd like to extend a special word of appreciation to Mike and Carolyn Parkinson. Besides your ongoing prayers on my behalf, you graciously allowed me to make use of your home at Lake Arrowhead to begin my writing. The beauty, the stillness, and God's peace I experienced there have taken permanent residence in my mind's eye. I really love you guys. Likewise, hats off to Dr. Bill Bright, Dr. Lloyd Olson, and my dear friends at Campus Crusade. The provision of a room and meals for several weeks at your lovely headquarters in Arrowhead Springs during the summer of 1991 provided the perfect setting for several chapters of my writing.

Then there's my hardworking research assistant, Darcy Nielsen. I especially appreciated her personal interest in the subject, not to mention the hours upon hours spent reading hundreds of newspaper clips and endless miles logged traveling from library to library. Darcy, I value your friendship.

It goes without saying that the greatest source of inspiration, prayer support, and ideas came from my marvelous family: Mom and Dad, Becky and Jack, Steve and Sharon, John and Alison, and brother Tim. I give thanks to the Lord for each one of you!

Finally, to Jesus, my best friend and Savior, thank You for setting the standard for our behavior and for the entertainment choices we make. Life would be impossible, not to mention miserable, without the means to discern right from wrong. Thank You for granting us the gift of discernment.

INTRODUCTION

While living in Los Angeles, I witnessed a rather curious phenomenon called the "bass car." The first time I encountered a bass car, I thought we were on the verge of an earthquake! In most cases you can hear—and in some instances actually *feel*—a bass car long before you see it coming. Named after the incredibly enormous, bass-heavy speaker systems, the driver of a bass car either assumes the entire world wants to share in his choice of music, or he's deaf. My guess is both are true.

If the bass car has yet to terrorize your neighborhood, perhaps you've been audibly assaulted by a youngster strutting down the street with a "boom box" on his shoulder. Oblivious to those around him, this future disc jockey pumps out the "jams" with piercing intensity, sure to create a migraine in the sturdiest armadillo. Then there's the kid next door. This guy's determined to become the next lead guitarist for Motley Crue. Whether it's day or night, your house is rocked with a sound that closely resembles a B-52 jet plane just before take-off.

"Turn that stuff down!" you may feel like shouting. And when push comes to shove, our kids do exactly that. With the aid of portable Sony Walkman-type tape players, a generation of children and teenagers have created a private world for listening to music—a world that's quieter for busy adults, but one that evades our scrutiny. When was the last time you considered what's playing in their headsets?

And consider the role of television in our homes. Life can be so hectic, and we're incredibly frazzled. "Just watch TV and leave me alone for a few minutes," we mumble. Dutifully, the children file out of our supervision and into the den. There, sitting before the family shrine in cushy chairs, they proceed to engage in a few hours of "vegging" and enlightenment before the guiding light of TV. There's nothing on? "No problem, kids. Pick anything you like from the video store." After all, with ten thousand selections they're sure to find *something*.

And indeed they will, but are all options available to them wise entertainment choices? *Perhaps not, but how bad could a video be at this "family" video outlet?* we wonder as we sit waiting in the car outside the store.

We've been told by "experts," by Hollywood's gurus, as well as the keepers of the media, that a teenager's involvement in popular music and film is a harmless part of their socialization. After all, we're talking about "entertainment," and that which entertains can't harm us. Or can it? Should parents care what their children see and hear? Has the cultural landscape really changed that much from when you and I were teens? Might music and media be influencing the actions and behavior of those who spend a lifetime consuming it?

Concerned parents are not the only folks cross-examining the culture these days. Even editors of national magazines have entered the exchange. For instance, three words dominated the April 1991 edition of *Newsweek:* "Violence Goes Mainstream." In this revealing essay, the authors analyzed our appetite for violence and destruction in movies, music, and books, and investigated the implications of our national entertainment diet. They inquired, "As America binges on make-believe gore, you have to ask: What are we doing to ourselves?"

After many discussions with school students, I have to wonder the same thing. In classrooms all across America, sitting nicely behind their desks, children and teens have described to me virtually every degrading form of entertainment imaginable, without batting an eye—entertainment which they find interesting, if not downright enjoyable. I've often wondered, *Why are young people filling their minds with this antisocial, contaminated material?* And on further reflection, I'm forced to ask, *Where are the parents?*

Frankly, I cannot remain on the sidelines watching this generation of youngsters feed their precious minds with self-destructive imagery. It's time we dusted off the lost art of discernment and played hard-ball with Hollywood's hype.

Who will benefit from this book? Parents, grandparents, educators, youth leaders—anyone who cares about the physical and spiritual well-being of the family, who feel as though the world of entertainment that daily invades the home is spinning out of control. Having teenage (or preteen) children is not a prerequisite. Newly engaged or young married couples will find this information a useful tool for securing a "head start" on their family's entertainment diet. In all the personal examples, I have changed the names of the people involved to protect their privacy.

You'll find that the first portion of our study addresses the emergence of a new "center of learning" which incorporates the industries of advertising, television and films, and music. In an eye-opening, just-as-

---

"A generation of children and teenagers have created a private world for listening to music—a world that's quieter for busy adults, but one that evades our scrutiny. When was the last time you considered what's playing in their headsets?"

---

your-children-see-it approach, we'll review the radical changes to the entertainment landscape—a transformation that has occurred right under our nose. The second portion provides the necessary steps to sharpen your skills of discernment. Likewise, we'll consider a practical blueprint to teach children how to "learn to discern."

Feeling powerless over what can be done about this base culture—or about what's playing in those pulsating "bass cars"? Read on.

PART ONE

MUSIC AND MEDIA: THE BATTLE FOR YOUNG MINDS

1 ASLEEP AT THE WHEEL

*I*t was a rude awakening for the quiet little town of Carl Junction, Missouri. In the nearby woods, three teenagers murdered a friend—partly out of curiosity—with baseball bats. Each of the boys had a particular interest in black metal music—music with lyrics that tell of torture and destruction. According to newspaper accounts, Jim Hardy, Ron Clements, and Pete Roland matter-of-factly stated that they wondered what it would feel like to kill someone. The victim, Steven Newberry, while being fatally clubbed to death, repeatedly asked his schoolmates, "Why me, you guys?" His friends replied, "Because it's fun, Steve."[1]

In April of 1989, Americans were shocked as reports of the savage rape and beating of a twenty-eight-year-old investment banker dominated the headlines. Unexplainably, a group of teenagers, ages fourteen to seventeen, went "wilding" (slang for a rampage of violence) in New York City's Central Park, a jaunt that left this banker virtually dead. Almost as frightening as the assault was a lack of remorse by these calloused attackers. When quizzed about the attack, fifteen-year-old Yusef Salaam told the district attorney's office, "It was fun."[2]

In January 1990, a twelve-year-old boy was convicted of raping his five-year-old stepsister. "He said he got the idea while watching TV at his aunt's house," explained Police Lt. Thomas Hull of San Leandro, California. Flipping through the channels, this adolescent stumbled on a program that showed an intimate lovemaking scene. "We don't know what the program was, whether it was an adult channel or a so-called soap opera," reported Lt. Hull. After the rape, when asked why he did it, the youngster told police, "It looked like fun."[3]

7

Did you notice the common thread weaving these unrelated events together? *Children* in a quest for *fun*—a good time, something to do. Nothing more. No big deal.

In the cases of Rod Matthews and Mark Branch the motive was different, but they achieved the same ghastly results. Matthews, a fifteen-year-old from Dedham, Massachusetts, repeatedly beat to death classmate Shaun Ouillette with a baseball bat on November 20, 1986. He drew inspiration from a videotape called *Faces of Death,* which, according to its producers, depicts *actual* death experiences. For Matthews, watching wasn't enough. He later explained to psychiatrists that he wanted to "see what it was like to kill someone."[4]

The motivation behind Mark Branch's story is similar. On October 24, 1988, the townspeople of Greenfield, Massachusetts, locked their doors tighter than ever before after news that this nineteen-year-old repeatedly stabbed eighteen-year-old Sharon Gregory. According to Police Chief David McCarthy, who investigated the case, a search of Branch's bedroom turned up a stack of *Friday the 13th* videotapes. His friends said that he was particularly fascinated with Jason, the slasher star of the *Friday* series. Chief McCarthy put it this way: "[Mark] wanted to see what it feels like to kill."[5]

"What blurred the picture of entertainment and reality in the mind of these youths?" "Didn't they know better?" "How could they become so hardened?" "What went wrong?" I watched with interest as members of the news media asked—in a state of shock, outrage, and disbelief— many questions as they attempted to cope with the moral decline of America's youth.

WIRED FOR SOUND

Having interviewed hundreds of students around the country about their entertainment diet, it's become painfully clear to me that the dispassionate attitudes of these young felons is not atypical. What's more, many "good kids" from "good homes" are just as much at risk. Three recent memories are worth sharing. At just ten-and-a-half years of age, Leah, a Christian school student, listed for me several episodes of *Friday the 13th* and *Porky's* among her all-time favorite films. Several other R-rated flicks made her list. I couldn't help wondering how a child barely eleven years old gained access to these films. (Keep in mind, they don't show these movies at her school.)

Take Byron. Outfitted with a Sony Walkman and a stack of cassette tapes, this eleven-year-old was wired for sound as we rode side by side on an airplane. Not wanting to pass up an opportunity to gain some primary data on the youth culture, I casually asked, "Byron, tell me about . . ." From favorite song lyrics to the latest video on MTV, for the next two hours Byron tired me out with exhaustive details about dozens of his favorite bands. His reason for enjoying explicit rap music—that the violence and abuse it described was "really cool"—was nothing short of chilling.

Finally, follow me into a classroom for a moment. I was asked to speak to a group of fifth graders in a private Christian school one hot afternoon. As I approached the room, I noticed the kids sleepily following along with the teacher in their math textbooks. As I entered the classroom, it took about a split second for these eyes to note the hockey mask in my hands.

Whispering in excited tones, several youngsters exclaimed, "That's Jason's mask!" The class came alive! Our discussion about Jason (the "star" from the teen horror film series *Friday the 13th*) and other movies during the next thirty minutes took little prompting to have complete audience participation. I still recall the teacher's face turning bright red as he witnessed his students describing ultimate acts of violent dismemberment and mutilation with startling accuracy. Afterward, he commented to me, "Bob, I've been in education for eighteen years, and unless I had been present to witness what took place today, I would have never believed it."

Looking back over these three encounters, I closed my eyes and reflected that Bob Dylan's prophetic song, "The times they are a changin'," was an understatement. There is no doubt in my mind that many of these precious kids have unknowingly taken a giant step in the direction of delinquency. As they provided me with justification for their choice of viewing, I couldn't help but wonder, *Where are their parents?* The thought struck me that we, the guardians of the next generation, appear to have fallen asleep, while our young speed blindly down the highway of moral decay.

I've noted three possible reasons for our extended nap. First, there's widespread denial that a problem exists in popular entertainment. Although we may concede that things are not perfect, we wrongly assume it can't be much worse than the era of Elvis shaking the nation with his pelvis. Second, we'd like to believe that teens are unacquainted with the excesses of Hollywood, so we hold on to a denial of any awareness. For those of us alert enough to recognize that, in fact, a problem does exist and that our children are plugged into their culture, we hope against hope that there is little impact upon behavior—a denial of influence. Satisfied that there really isn't anything to be alarmed about, that our children somehow have a protective bubble which keeps them innocent, and that, in the event they do discover degrading entertainment imagery, no harm is done, we roll over for another snooze.

Meanwhile, children around the country are waking up to a culture that teaches them to equate violence with a good time. For instance, in November of 1990, over ten thousand kids responded to a survey on media violence conducted by Mindworks, a division of the *Star Tribune* in Minneapolis, Minnesota. According to the newspaper, among the most common refrains was, "I love violence. Violence is cool."

Mindworks reported that the young writers responding to their poll (grades 1–12) "described with delight bludgeonings, brains splattering, and blood streaming everywhere." Furthermore, "Their essays overflowed with tales of legs splitting in two, throats being ripped open, and heads rolling down stairs. They offered visions of people being chopped, squashed, slashed, and annihilated by every means possible." Tom Klimisch, a high school senior, was quoted as saying, "When I watch someone getting beat up, it just makes me feel good inside."[6]

Even the American Medical Association has voiced concerns about the pulse of popular media.[7] During the summer of 1990, the AMA adopted a statement regarding destructive themes contained in some contemporary music. Dr. William C. Scott, chairman of the AMA Council on Scientific Affairs, explained that certain types of music "may present a real threat to the physical health and emotional well-being of especially vulnerable children and adolescents." Of greatest potential harm was music that advocated drug and alcohol abuse, suicide, satanic worship, sexual exploitation, and racism. The AMA report cited evidence that these themes may be associated with social isolation or may even lead to "active participation in, or passive acceptance of, destructive behaviors" among adolescents.

SNOOZE, YOU LOSE

In some ways our predicament is much like that of Rip Van Winkle. One lazy afternoon he took a drink and fell asleep under a tree. When he awoke, unbeknown to him, twenty years had passed. In his absence, the village was transfigured. All that he loved was suddenly gone. Rip was alone in a world that he could not comprehend.

Unlike Rip's story, what we'll be examining in the following pages is not a fairy tale. While we were asleep at the wheel, our cultural landscape was transformed into a bad dream of nightmarish proportions. It appears that our high-tech world of home video machines has produced a generation of morally numb users. Does that sound a bit alarmist? A tad overstated? Is it really that bad?

Consider the report filed by the United States Senate Judiciary Committee in March of 1991 that concluded that the United States is "the most violent and self-destructive nation on earth." Noting that the U.S. population had grown by 41 percent since 1960, it found violent crimes

> *"While we were asleep at the wheel, our cultural landscape was transformed into a bad dream of nightmarish proportions. It appears that our high-tech world of home video machines has produced a generation of morally numb users."*

increasing a whopping 516 percent during the same period. Further, the report documented that in 1990 "the United States led the world with its murder, rape, and robbery rates."[8] In the words of Ronald Reagan, "Facts are stubborn things."

Can there be any doubt that the moral fabric of American society is unraveling?

Who's to blame? In 1990, in the midst of a deteriorating social order, songwriter Billy Joel struck a responsive chord with the popular hit, "We Didn't Start the Fire." In effect, Joel (who was many years older than the teens he was attempting to identify with) was saying: Don't blame this generation for the problems of today; what's gone wrong has been wrong since the beginning of time.

His don't-put-the-blame-on-us message reminds me of a parent who, while attempting to come to terms with the delinquency of his own child, explained: "My kid's all screwed up from heavy metal music and exposure to sexual videos on MTV at an early age. You can't blame *me* for his problems. I'm never home!" Hmmm. Whether a rock star or just a parent caught between a rock and a hard place, it appears no one wants to admit he might possibly be negligent.

So, who is responsible for the crumbling character of our children?[9] Although I believe there are several powerful external forces at work, frankly I am convinced that you and I—the folks who ought to be providing our children with moral and spiritual leadership—are ultimately at fault. There, I said it. Not the best way to start a book. After all, it would be easy to lay the blame at the feet of Hollywood.

And it's understandable that we might want to point the finger at the long-haired, hot-blooded rock star wearing last week's fishnet stocking who has our kids worked into a regular frenzy. Don't get me wrong. I recognize that the "anything goes" music and media diet that our nation consumes is causing severe moral and spiritual indigestion. That's why a significant portion of this book will examine the powerful "voices" of the popular entertainment culture. However, during our examination of these external forces, don't lose sight of the fact that the buck stops here—with you and me.

"EDUTAINMENT"

So, what do I mean by "voices"? There was a time in American history when the primary centers of learning were three in number: the school, the church, and the home. If your child was placed in a suitable school, if he was involved in a good church program, and given the fact that you supervised what was taking place at home, you could rest assured that your bases were covered.

Today, however, there is a fourth center of learning: the world of popular entertainment personified in a chorus of "voices." These voices include the music industry, television and film industries, advertising, comic books, video games, and the news media. Even though they come wrapped in the innocent package called *entertainment,* all are capable of transmitting values, morals, ideologies, and attitudes about life in bigger-than-life terms. This combination of education and entertainment could be called *edutainment.* Recent technological breakthroughs—VCRs, Sony Walkman-type portable tape players, cable television, and consumer satellite dishes (all developed within the last two decades)—are now common household items that serve as the message bearers of this fourth center of learning.

My experience working with children would indicate that they are frequently more tuned in to these voices than their classroom instruction, the church, or their home. Hard to believe? Take, for instance, the National Coalition on Television Violence survey of 100 students ages ten to thirteen years old in the suburb of Champaign, Illinois, that discovered that Freddy Krueger (the slasher film star from *Nightmare on Elm Street*) was better known than many famous American leaders. Brace yourself: 66 percent could correctly identify Freddy Krueger, while only 36 percent knew that Abraham Lincoln was a president of the United States.[10]

Another reason children are so acquainted with slasher stars can be attributed to the media attention which elevates fictional mass-murders to star status. For example, Tom Bradley, mayor of Los Angeles—a city of twelve million people—proclaimed September 13, 1991, as "Freddy Krueger day." It appears that the mayor caved in to industry pressure to applaud a "star" who makes his living killing innocent people on the silver screen.

In a letter defending his ludicrous pronouncement, Bradley explained, "When I was asked to proclaim Friday the thirteenth for this film character, I knew this was a way to thank New Line Cinema for supporting Los Angeles. More importantly, I knew these series of films have been a fantasy creation of Hollywood and in no way have been based on real events."

Of course, the good mayor failed to do his homework on that point. Robert England, the actor who plays Freddy Krueger, *has* confessed in slasher film magazines, such as *Slaughter House,* that he drew inspiration and ideas from real-life mass murderer Ted Bundy. Bradley further justified himself, stating, "The youngsters who have seen these films understand the huge distinction between a fantasy film and reality."[11] (One wonders what psychological data he's using to back up that assertion.)

Further evidence of this familiarity with the voices of the pop culture hit home for me through an offhanded comment made by my research assistant, Darcy Nielsen. In preparation for this book, I asked Darcy to read through a thousand letters I've received from junior highers—letters with questions about specific music groups or films. Having plowed through the mail bag, in a note to me Darcy commented, "It is sad to admit, but today's teens appear to be lacking in good communication and writing skills. Letter after letter contained misspelled words and fragmented sentences." What really struck me came next: "The only things which the teens *always* had correct were lyrics copied down from popular songs or the names of a band and their album titles."

While parents are hard at work to provide for their families, due to a lack of energy many spend little time with the kids. By default, this void allows the popular entertainment culture to serve as chief baby-sitter. I'll never forget the words of Gary Bauer, president of the Family Research Council in Washington, D.C., while serving as the White House domestic policy advisor for President Reagan. He once observed: "What are we saying to our children if we allow them to spend more time watching television by the time they are six than they will spend talking with their fathers the rest of their lives?"

In our absence, this fourth center of learning works around the clock inculcating children with values often at odds with our Judeo-Christian heritage. For example, there are many biblical passages upholding sexual restraint. However, the virtue of virginity, if you will, is a foreign concept to our American youth culture. In fact, more often than not, virginity is mocked.

Several years ago, I was leading a discussion about popular music with fourth graders at a private Christian school on this very topic. With an embarrassed giggle, one youngster asked if Madonna's hit song, "Like A Virgin," was good or bad. Unsure how much fourth grade students knew about sex, I asked the class to define *virgin* in order to answer their inquiry. Sally explained, "It's a girl who doesn't do sex." I see. "Can boys be virgins, too?" I asked. In one of those priceless moments, with hand outstretched Mark exclaimed, *"I am, I am!"* My first thought was, *Only in the fourth grade would anyone freely, confidently, and proudly wear that label.*

"We may encourage them to say no to sex, but the entertainment industry pounds the message of the joys of promiscuity into young minds virtually every day."

By contrast, let me share two angry letters from junior highers who took exception to a column I wrote wherein I challenged the sexual attitudes of several popular musicians. In defense of the lead singer of Guns N' Roses, Carey wrote, "I think if Axl Rose wants to have sex through every waking hour that's just fine. . . . I don't think there is anything wrong with premarital sex as long as the people involved have no objections." Jenna stated, "How can you say premarital sex is a sin! You and every other guy in the world wouldn't be able to withstand not having sex until marriage, let alone waiting until after the age of sixteen." She added several choice words to make her point. Suffice it to say that Jenna, Carey, and probably more adolescents than we'd like to imagine, have embraced the notion that remaining a virgin until marriage is an impossible, even undesirable goal.

Can we blame them for feeling this way? We may encourage them to say no to sex, but the entertainment industry pounds the message of the joys of promiscuity into young minds virtually every day. For example, over the last ten years of speaking to youth, I've challenged thousands of teens to name *just one song* that they've heard on top-forty radio which says, in effect, that waiting to have sex until marriage is a good idea, a noble ideal, or even a possibility.

Typically, I'll offer a twenty-dollar reward if anyone can come up with *one* song. Sadly, nobody in ten years has been able to identify such a tune (on secular radio). As far as my research goes, when it comes to secular hit radio there has never been a song in the top forty that upholds the virtues of virginity. When a child makes a commitment to honor the Lord with his or her body—to treat the gift of virginity with loving care and respect—his or her decision will, in most cases, not be reinforced by what he or she sees on television or at the movies or hears in popular music. We've grown accustomed to giving this powerful fourth information center free reign in our homes.

LEARNING TO DISCERN

In many respects, we find ourselves in a situation much like that of the people of Israel in the Old Testament. The Lord, speaking through the prophet Ezekiel, said of His chosen people: "They have made no distinction between the holy and the profane, and they have not taught the difference between the unclean and the clean" (22:26). They, like us, failed to equip their families with proper discernment skills and an appreciation for righteousness. When we as a nation overlook the important task of sharpening our children's discerning skills, it should come as no surprise when youth act out some of the powerfully painted fantasies of deviant behavior which so dominate the entertainment they consume.

You may be thinking, *Oh, but my family is different. I do restrict what the kids watch and listen to. How can this book be of value to me?* There is a world of difference between restricting access to unwholesome material (which is an important first step) and teaching kids to *think* for themselves. Take, for example, the last time you noticed the kids watching an offensive scene on TV. If you're like most, you may have said something along the lines of, "I want you to turn that television show off—*now!*" What's the first response you get from your youngsters? Usually, with a whine in their voices, they ask, "But why?" Have you ever heard yourself fire back with a shout, "Because I said so! End of discussion"?

In the heat of the moment, we've missed an important opportunity to maximize an object lesson in discernment. It's easy to fall into the trap of building a huge cage around our kids to protect them. We give them a long "don't watch—don't listen to" list. Unfortunately, when children outgrow the cage we've designed for them, or when they are not directly under our supervision, they don't have the tools to make good choices on their own.

Thus, our goal in the pages that follow can be summed up with this simple phrase: Learn to discern. Using Proverbs 3:21(NIV) as our mandate—"My son, preserve sound judgment and discernment, do not let them out of your sight"—we'll examine what I consider the three most

---

"When we as a nation overlook the important task of sharpening our children's discerning skills, it should come as no surprise when youth act out some of the powerfully painted fantasies of deviant behavior which so dominate the entertainment they consume."

---

powerful media voices: advertising, television and film, and music. I feel certain that you'll discover several key aspects of the media assault on our youth that you never knew were operative. After our "crash course" of problematic trends in advertising, movies, and music, we'll explore a number of step-by-step strategies to help you regain lost ground in the home. Several chapters are dedicated to providing practical advice on how to assist teens as they seek to sharpen their discernment skills. Don't let the first few chapters which document the problem discourage you to the point of despair. Help is around the corner!

As I set out to chronicle the media's destructiveness, there will be times that you will be offended by the images or lyrical passages I've cited to illustrate my point. I understand those feelings. Believe me, I've wrestled with this issue for many years. Because I firmly believe that every parent needs to see *at least once* what eight- and ten-year-old young people are viewing and hearing virtually every day, my original intention was not to edit any of the images or lyrics in the pages ahead. After all, since nobody is sanitizing the entertainment culture for our children, I didn't think that I should sanitize it for adult readers. I believe that you and I can't fully appreciate the problem without exposure to some small part of it, as difficult a process as that may be.

As mentioned earlier, there is widespread denial that a problem exists at all. The best way to fully comprehend the problems within the youth culture and break down the walls of denial is to consider the evidence firsthand. However, since I believe that many adult readers would be too offended by an unedited version of our children's world, you'll notice that we've blackened out portions of various photos and abbreviated much of the vulgarities. But bear in mind that the messages and images our young people receive are not tampered with in this manner. Again, let me apologize in advance for the offensive nature of some of the examples, even in this edited form. Please keep in mind that nothing we will examine in this book was found in a pornographic bookstore.

In studying this book, you'll soon learn that many periodicals which clutter our coffee tables—magazines like *Good Housekeeping, Glamour,* and *Cosmopolitan*—from time to time carry advertisements as explicit as the centerfold of *Playboy.* You'll gain a new appreciation for the antiporn groups that are working to clean up cable television. The very cable companies that we allowed to wire our neighborhoods together now pump R- and X-rated films into our living rooms. And we'll turn up the volume on the music that plays in the private world of our children's headphones. After that I think you may agree with me that if Elvis were alive today, he'd blush at the gyrations of modern musicians.

I'd like to point out that entire books have been written on the three voices—advertising, television and films, and music. As such, my intention is not to offer you a comprehensive exposé of these individual fields of study. Rather, I'll provide you with some historical perspective as well as a status report of current events to set the stage for our ultimate goal: "Learn to discern." And remember, it's never too early to start teaching children to think critically and "Christianly" about all forms of media. In fact, the earlier you activate the process, the better. Don't laugh. Beginning to teach four-year-olds how to think critically will help prevent them from becoming traditional American couch potatoes!

Children are not born as moral mutants unable to help who they are. God has placed His imprint upon every man's conscience. Since the habits of your children's hearts are shaped by what plays in the theater of their minds, we must work with diligence to help them fix their thoughts "on things above." This process (as you probably already know) is one of life's greatest challenges. I believe the legacy you will create can also be one of life's most rewarding opportunities.

So without further delay, fasten your seat belt as we take a closer look at the challenges facing this generation at risk. And may God awaken our sleeping hearts.

2 MADISON AVENUE: SELLING TEENS SHORT

*I*f you're like me, you probably consider advertising the lowest form of human communication. It's unwanted; it interrupts our TV program, our reading, our thinking. If you're like me, you probably find that many ads insult our intelligence. Oh, sure, from time to time there are a few that make us smile. Some advertisements are creative, in an offbeat way. Admittedly I turn up the radio to hear the country twang of Tom Bodett as he reminds us, "At Motel 6, we'll leave the light on." And I get a kick out of hearing those good ol' boys from Bartle and Jaymes say, "We thank you for your support." But, by and large, ads are a hassle.

Like it or not, we live in a world saturated with advertising. It's on our clothing, buses, trucks, billboards, TV and radio, and in magazines and newspapers. And if you visit the beach, inevitably somebody will fly overhead in a small plane with an ad banner in tow. Unless you're a hermit, it's practically impossible to go a day without seeing a few dozen ads. No wonder I've come to observe a curious habit in more than one household. Perhaps you've seen someone do it; maybe you've even done it. I'm referring to *the way* folks watch television. The moment a commercial comes on—zap! They change the channel and watch several shows at the same time! After all, few of us tune in to watch all of those silly commercials.

Because we hate commercial messages, it's easy to dismiss them as unworthy of serious study. Furthermore, we may underestimate the impact that ads actually have on us and our children. This, as we shall see, can have subtle but far-reaching consequences.

But wait a minute—can advertising really influence us, our spending habits and the products we buy? The makers of Diet Coke, Isuzu pickup trucks, Slice soft drink, and the Foot Locker think they can; they were among the sponsors who each paid six hundred thousand dollars for one thirty-second commercial during Super Bowl XXI. They spent twenty thousand dollars *per second* to parade their products before the eyes of an estimated one hundred thirty million viewers in *hopes* of bringing new customers to the register. Believe me, it was more than a hope! You don't throw half a million dollars around unless you are fairly confident that your ad will produce results.

If you are skeptical about the ability of an advertiser to position its product in your mind, take this brief quiz and fill in the blank where I've left out the product name or key word in the ad slogan.

1. "You deserve a break today at _____ ."

2. Three older ladies in a Wendy's commercial asked, "Where's the _____ ?"

3. Mr. Whipple sternly asks supermarket shoppers, "Please don't squeeze the _____ ."

4. "When E. F. Hutton speaks, people _____ ."

5. "M-m m-m good. That's what _____ soup is, m-m m-m good."

How did you score? Over the last several years, I've asked audiences to fill in those blanks. Amazingly on average, 90 percent of the crowd will shout out the correct answers: McDonald's, beef, Charmin, listen, and Campbell's. Think about that. I give an unannounced quiz on a subject nobody's studied, and the majority pass the test. That's *powerful*. And that is also why I don't think we can afford to turn the page too quickly on this important voice of the culture. After all, if Madison Avenue can sell us hamburgers, jeans, and automobiles in thirty-second chunks of time, what else might we be buying? That is, is it possible our values are also influenced and shaped by advertisers?

A PICTURE IS WORTH A THOUSAND WORDS

To answer that question—what else might we be buying—here are three keys to the inner workings of advertising. The first key: built into every ad is a *strategy of persuasion*. In the case of print and television ads, this strategy of persuasion relies heavily on images—images designed to appeal to our *feelings*. For example, a recent McDonald's commercial depicts a father and young daughter happily driving together to the

---

"Because we hate commercial messages, it's easy to dismiss them as unworthy of serious study. Furthermore, we may underestimate the impact that ads actually have on us and our children."

"golden arches" for lunch. With smiles on their faces, this duo sits by the playground feeding each other french fries as the sun shines brightly overhead. Laughter is in the air. It's a "feel good" commercial.

Because the ad appeals to our feelings, we're discouraged from thinking about what we're seeing. In fact, asking critical questions about this kind of ad is virtually impossible. Will some (or all) dads who take their six-year-olds to McDonald's experience this happiness? There's really no way to know. Instead, we consumers must judge a given ad on whether or not the image appeals to us. Do I like what I see? Do I desire to have that same warm experience associated with eating a french fry? These are our considerations, not, is it right or wrong, true or false, likely or unlikely. The commercial becomes an *aesthetic* experience.

A second key to advertising is that consumers, including you and me, instinctively treat photographs and video pictures as *reality*. What we see we believe to be real, accurate, and truthful. After all, most of us have taken pictures with a pocket camera. What we get back from the developer is pretty much what we saw when we shot the photo. Not so in the world of advertising. Rarely does an ad slick appear in a magazine without some degree of retouching, especially when we're talking about a model. Sometime when you have a free afternoon, you should visit an art studio that does photo retouching. Right before your eyes you see skin blemishes removed, eye color adjusted, stray hair hidden, and even crooked smiles straightened.

In essence, our innocent view of pictures has been exploited by the advertising industry. We trust that what we're seeing is genuine. But in the world of advertising, reality has been touched up, edited, shaded, colored, and designed to represent something other than what is real. Co-authors Al Ries and Jack Trout in *Positioning: The Battle for Your Mind* explain why this is so: "One prime objective of all advertising is to heighten expectations. To create the illusion that the product or service will perform the miracles you expect."[1] By and large, advertising is a fantasy world that plays upon our needs, fears, wants, and desires, promising miracle cures for what ails us.

The third key to the way advertising works lies in the idea of *double think*. With one side of our brain, we discern that what we're seeing is a fantasy. There's just no way that dozens of beautiful women will swoon if we splash brand-X cologne on our face. Intellectually, we know the implied promise of this ad is false. But, at the same time, we'd like to think that maybe, just maybe, the chances of turning heads would be increased if we wore brand-X, and so with the other side of our brains we embrace the hope "that it might just work." That's double think.

Understanding these three concepts—that advertisements contain a strategy of persuasion, that people instinctively (yet wrongly) trust that what they see is real, and that we're to some degree victims of double think—will help you understand why we can be so influenced by the ad images we consume. Television news journalist Bill Moyers explored this matter in a detailed documentary for the Public Broadcasting System (PBS) in 1989 entitled, "Consuming Images." His study found the average American consumes more than thirty-two thousand commercials annually (at that rate we'd consume over a million commercials by age thirty-five). He also pointed out that in 1988 alone, more than $110 billion was spent on TV and print advertising. If advertising didn't work, why advertise?

Personally, if our discussion on advertising was limited to the way we're manipulated into buying a specific breakfast cereal, I'd say skip the balance of this chapter. After all, knowing "four out of five dentists" recommend my brand of toothpaste is heartwarming. However, the significance of our study is far more consequential. As you'll see in a moment, matters of self-worth and a proper understanding of human sexuality are aspects of life which the advertising industry directly impacts. Author and lecturer Stuart Ewen (Hunter College, New York) recognizes our need to improve our "visual literacy." He observes, "From

> *"Matters of self-worth and a proper understanding of human sexuality are aspects of life which the advertising industry directly impacts."*

very early on, students need to be educated into the idea that images speak, that images say certain kinds of things, that there are values, priorities, and meanings imbedded in these images. They need to learn about the vocabulary and grammar of images."[2]

Because the images imbedded in the ads we consume can shape the patterns of who we become, what we dress like, look like, smell like, and so on, it's important to answer our previous question—what else might we be buying? For the purposes of this book, we'll limit our discussion to two areas of concern: ads that undermine the self-esteem of our daughters and advertisements that sell us a warped picture of human sexuality.

COSMETIC FIXATION

Take a quick glance into any adolescent girl's bedroom, and what do you usually find—ad pages torn out of fashion and life-style magazines such as *Teen, Glamour, Cosmopolitan, Elle,* or *Vogue.* Why do they do this? Is something wrong with their parents' choice of wallpaper? The ads provide teen eyes with a map of what's hot and what's not. Actually, these images are more than a map. They represent the standard by which an impressionable teen will measure herself.

In his book *The Strong Family,* Chuck Swindoll colorfully describes the feelings adolescent girls wrestle with as they compare themselves to this false standard. He writes, "Each tiny zit assures her that leprosy is just around the corner. And clothes? We're talking daily nervous breakdown. And she's got this body that won't make up its mind . . . plus the kids at school and the commercials on the tube and the magazines in the rack all team up in some kind of secret conspiracy that convinces your once easygoing little lass she is horribly overweight, ugly beyond belief, and hopelessly condemned to a life of embarrassment."[3]

In 1990, the pop music band Roxette hit it big with their song "She's Got the Look," an anthem of sorts for kids in search of the ultimate pose. Some of my female readers will understand from firsthand experience this concept of getting "the look." After all, at thirty-seven you're still trying to get the look. My advice: Give it up! Go easy on the family budget for a while and stop spending money needlessly. Relax. In the words of Proverbs 31:30 (TEV), "Charm is deceptive and beauty disappears, but a woman who fears the LORD should be praised."

So, ladies, why might you (and your daughters) be tempted to compare yourself against these retouched photo images? Along the way, someone probably made a comment about your slightly different nose, your eye color, breast size, the length of your legs—all things that you have absolutely no control over. But forever you feel pressure to compensate for these alleged inadequacies. The picture is further clouded by the false standard that the fashion and beauty industry has raised. For example, the cover of *Mademoiselle* once featured this story: "Breasts That Measure Up." According to the editors, what is important?—who you are as an individual on the *inside,* or what you look like on the *outside?*

By comparing oneself to this false standard, an individual is robbed of self-esteem and personal contentment. Remember, it's to the advantage of an advertiser if every time you look in the mirror you get the nagging message: *You don't measure up!* The advertiser, of course, has the solution to your problem. No two-page ad makes my point better than this spread from Merle Norman. On the first page (see figure 2.1), Ms. Average Josephine asks a lot of questions: "How can I make my square face appear more oval? How can I shape my lips and have a sexier mouth? Can I really learn to contour my face so I have dramatic-looking cheekbones?"

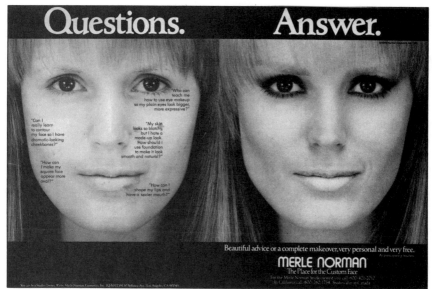

Figure 2.1: Picture-perfect results promised with these products.

Page two provides the solution to these questions: Come to Merle Norman for a makeover. But wait just a minute. Why is an oval face more attractive than square? If everyone had an oval face, how would you stand out in a crowd with your own special look? Who's to say exactly what a "dramatic-looking cheekbone" is shaped like, anyway?

An ad for L'Oreal's Plenitude promises to reduce the "signs of aging." Lancôme of Paris has the answer for cellulite. A firm from California, BeautySystems, offers us the ultimate: "Now you can have the body you've always wanted." Just pick up their body gel and massager to tone up all over. Or, if you're so mad about your eye color that you can't see straight, how about this ad for Softcolors by Ciba. The headline reads: "Introducing the eyes you wish you had been born with."

Then there's The Invisible Concealer by Cover Girl (see figure 2.2). By using this product, "undereye circles, tiny lines, facial flaws vanish from sight."

It's amazing the extremes we go to in order to hide the realities of life—we're imperfect and we're getting older. Can you think of anyone who isn't? So what are we doing to ourselves? Stuart Ewen believes "a lot of what all this is about is the construction of a front which will, in fact, be a viable, sellable front for public consumption."[4] Is it any wonder that teenage girls invest so much money in their image, spending a small fortune on the name brands which line their closets. I believe the "front" they are constructing and the look they're striving for comes at the expense of who they are.

Before you dismiss me as a male who just doesn't understand these things, please understand I certainly applaud a person looking and feeling her or his best. But there is a world of difference between good skin care and the unhealthy obsession with cosmetics.

Figure 2.2: Some products take cosmetics to an unhealthy obsessive level.

How can we help our daughters (or granddaughters) understand the difference amid the shouts to the contrary from the communications jungle? Chapter 6 provides a number of suggestions.

MADISON AVENUE BARES ALL

"Sex sells." That's probably why so many advertisers rely on sexual themes to hype their products. During the decade of the eighties, some advertisers turned that phrase around and began to "sell sex." Or perhaps I should say they began to sell us a warped perspective of human sexuality. Members of the advertising community have incorporated explicit nudity along with the themes of fornication, group sex, lesbianism—even rape—into their ad strategy. Keep in mind, these deviant sexual themes have inherently little to do with the product offered.

As you study the following, you may wonder, *Who's behind this?* Frankly, I have my doubts that this is some sort of grand scheme by liberal Madison Avenue ad gurus to indoctrinate society with their sexual agenda. However, I wouldn't hesitate for a minute to believe that

---

"I wouldn't hesitate for a minute to believe that individuals in positions of influence have used, and will continue to use, their power to shape public opinion on what is normal sexual behavior."

---

individuals in positions of influence have used, and will continue to use, their power to shape public opinion on what is normal sexual behavior. For example, when the AIDS crisis throws cold water on the gay movement, what better way to elevate and reshape the public's perception of homosexuality than through an ad which subtly presents lesbianism as normative and desirable?

Take photographer Bruce Weber, for instance. He's the forty-five-year-old cameraman behind Calvin Klein's explicit and often sexually deviant advertisements. In the early eighties, his controversial ads began to turn up in magazines and on billboards nationwide. Weber explains, "We're going through an extremely repressive period right now, and, partly because of AIDS, young people aren't free to experiment and find out what their own true sexual identity might be. Consequently, sexual images are particularly important right now. People mustn't be prohibited from looking at them because that kind of control breeds sickness into society."[5] As part of his sexual agenda, Weber popularized ads featuring muscular young men wearing only snug-fitting jockey shorts, later to explore openly homoerotic and group sex pictures.

Whether or not there exists an orchestrated attempt to inculcate society with these sexual perspectives is really not the issue. The fact is that children today are easily introduced to immoral ideas about their sexuality, and discerning parents must help them steer clear of them. As we chronicle the crude edge of contemporary advertising, please keep in mind that *none* of the ads were purchased from an adult bookstore; rather, all of them were contained in magazines that routinely clutter our coffee tables. I firmly believe that the reason why advertisers are successfully marketing these degrading pictures of the gift of sex is because you and I haven't seen the evidence for ourselves.

Picture This

No advertiser in recent times has included more deviant sexual themes than Calvin Klein. And that's not an accident. Consider for a moment the agenda of Calvin Klein's controversial cameraman Bruce Weber: "One of the wonderful things about photographs is that they can make people wonder about their own sexuality because people tend to read photographs in a way that pertains to their fantasy life."[6] Weber *wants* us to wonder about our sexual expression, and Calvin Klein products provide the backdrop. There's little doubt that this approach to advertising irrevocably changed the boundaries of what is considered acceptable in fashion advertising.

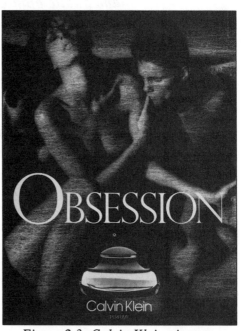

Figure 2.3: Calvin Klein pioneers group sex images in advertisements.

You've probably seen this Obsession ad at one time or another (see figure 2.3). Not only was it featured in the pages of fashion magazines, it was also used as a billboard. I can still remember seeing it on a billboard in downtown Pittsburgh in the fall of 1986. Driving past the billboard, I marveled at the fact that this billboard in a prominent public place featured group sex and went unchallenged. "Group sex?" you say. Take a closer look. In the center we see what appears to be a naked woman who is being sexually aroused by a naked man on her right. Look again. On her left there's a second guy. Notice the side shot of his leg by the letters "Obs" in Obsession. Once you've identified it, look directly above his leg and to the left of her shoulder. You'll find the right side profile of his face, ear, jawbone, and neck.

Other Calvin Klein ads with the theme of group sex are not so hard to identify. Consider this Calvin Klein Sport ad (see figure 2.4). What is really being sold here? What is the "sport" that Klein is suggesting? What does this deviant behavior have to do with clothing or fashion?

Figure 2.4: Calvin Klein portrays group sex as a "sport."

Part of Weber and Klein's sexual agenda appears to be intentionally confusing and purposefully leaving the encounter open to suggestion (see figure 2.5). What does this ad suggest to you? Why are they both naked? Were they having sex in the park? Was this woman raped? Abducted? Clearly, they were not just out for a stroll. At a more elementary level, what might this ad communicate about the public display of nudity?

In 1989, Calvin Klein further undressed our standard of decency with his ad for Obsession (as featured in *Cosmopolitan*). It appears we, as a nation, have lost the ability to blush (see figure 2.6).

Lest you feel your family is safe from these explicit advertisements because you don't allow the likes of *Glamour* and *Cosmopolitan* into your home, I must point something out. The following ad for Nivea products was originally sent to me by a mother who spotted it in *Good Housekeeping* in 1989 (see figure 2.7).

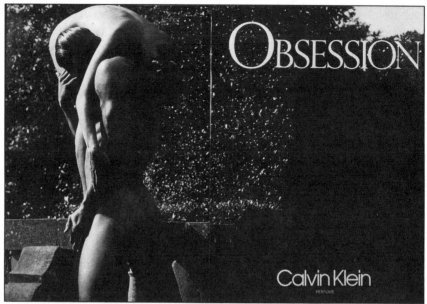

Figure 2.5: Calvin Klein's sexual agenda purposefully leaves this encounter open to the suggestion of rape.

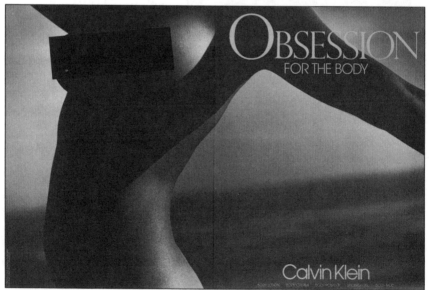

Figure 2.6: Undressing the public's standard of decency, this ad originally appeared in several magazines with no black outs.

Hard to believe, isn't it? That was the exact reaction of many *Good Housekeeping* subscribers. The ad raised so much flack, the editors promised readers they wouldn't publish the ad again.

Unfortunately, this yo-yoing back and forth between self-restraint in advertising and the overt commercialization of sex has created a society that is desensitized to indecency. Let me demonstrate exactly how far we've slid into the sewer. The following is a copy of the centerfold from the January 1957 issue of *Playboy* magazine (see figure 2.8). Think about it. Today, some

Figure 2.7: When Good Housekeeping displayed this Nivea ad (without black outs) many readers threatened to cancel their subscriptions.

Figure 2.8: This centerfold from Playboy magazine is less explicit than some ads today.

advertisements are more explicit than this centerfold from a porno magazine in the year that I was born. Like Rip Van Winkle, we've been asleep, sleeping while the visual landscape of American advertising has been radically transformed.

What has snapped in the judgment of corporate America to permit this continual exploitation of sex and women? What are children learning from the powerful sexual images they meet at younger and younger ages? Certainly they'll learn that modesty is outmoded. After the doors of decency were knocked off their hinges in the eighties, a small tidal wave of explicit ads sailed into our living rooms reinforcing that notion. Chanel N° 5, Zena Jeans, Halston, Guess, and Jordache have all presented women in various stages of undress.

What's Wrong with This Picture?

Explicit sex in advertising aside, evaluate for a moment several other warped perspectives of human sexuality presented by ad makers in the eighties and nineties. The theme of homosexual and lesbian love is a fairly new development. Take, for example, this ad (see figure 2.9) for Grand Passion which says, "In life there are many loves, but only one Grand Passion." What is the setting? A hotel bedroom. Did you notice the primary people are both women dressed in night garments— one has on a silk slip, the other pajamas. By implication, the consumer infers that lesbianism might certainly be one of life's legitimate passions.

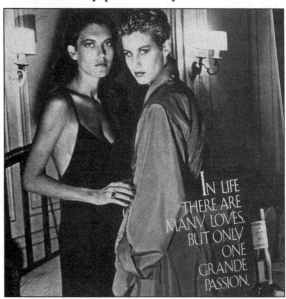

Figure 2.9: Grand Passion liquor incorporates the lesbian sex theme in their ads.

When we study advertising and find that group sex, homosexual ideas, and blatant nudity are prevalent, it's easy to lose sight that plain, old-fashioned, premarital sex is—certainly from God's perspective—out of bounds. If a child is determined to honor God by remaining a virgin until marriage, this decision will be at odds with the images and ad messages he or she will see throughout his or her formative years.

During the fall of 1985, the Swatch Watch company crafted a multi-page ad series which they placed in virtually every magazine targeting teen girls (see figure 2.10). On the first page we see a rather hip looking girl on her car phone. Page two pictures a guy, possibly summoned by the girl, traveling in an awful hurry. The next page these two are seen "swatchin' in the rain." But wait, there's more. Following two pages displaying various Swatch products, on page six the guy "puts the move" on her. We then find the couple, on page seven, at one of their apartments perhaps. The ad reads: "It's time to trust me."

In the final page of this Swatch affair (at no time are the individuals pictured with wedding bands), we find the passionate couple in bed together. Note the slogan: "Swatch—It's about time?" How many different things might that phrase mean? Certainly on the surface it could be

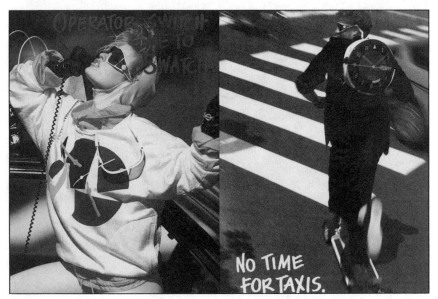

Figure 2.10: Swatch is selling much more than watches in this ad series.

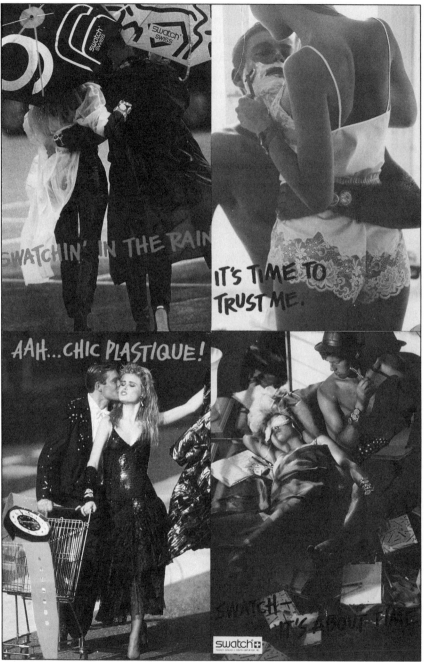

Figure 2.10 continued

argued that it means "Swatch sells more than watches." But the aggressive encounter and sexual buildup could also change the meaning to "Isn't it about time you went for it?" If what you want is to "handle a hunk" or pick up a "hip chick," the implied message is that Swatch has what it takes.

If you think I might be reading into that, perhaps my next example will be more straightforward. I have yet to find an ad that promotes the joys of fornication more overtly than this advertisement by Kads Clothing (see figure 2.11). Here we see the same man putting the "move" on *nine* different women. The ad reads, "So many women, so little time."

What does this ad suggest to men? How about: life is short, live it to the fullest by "scoring" with as many women as time permits. (Incidentally, the behavior of basketball star Wilt Chamberlain is reminiscent of this ad's irresponsible message. Chamberlain boasted in late 1991 of engaging in sex with more than twenty thousand women.) It's a takeoff on the old beer commercial—"You only go around once in life, so grab for all of the gusto." And what might an advertisement like this imply to women? How about: you exist to satisfy a man's sexual exploration. Borrowing a concept popularized by singer Madonna, this ad reduces women to nothing more than a "Boy Toy."

Figure 2.11: Kads Clothing encourages promiscuity and exploitation of women.

Certainly there can be no doubt about the message of fornication and sexploitation by this advertiser—an offense to all who share the Judeo-Christian heritage. But there's another side to this. We're living in an era where more than thirty-three thousand cases of sexually transmitted diseases (STDs) are reported to the Centers for Disease Control *every single day*. That number is an understated picture of the problem because it only includes those cases of STDs that are *reported*. In light

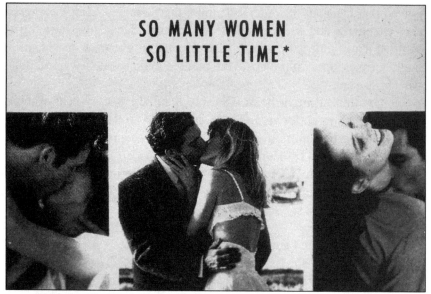

Figure 2.12: Kads promotes multiple partners even with 33,000 cases of sexually transmitted disease reported every day.

of that alarming fact, is this advertiser acting in a socially responsible manner with its "so many women, so little time" ad pitch?

If you look closely, next to the slogan you'll see an asterisk (see figure 2.12). At the bottom of the ad, in small print, they advise: "Be careful" (see figure 2.13). Oh, I see. It's okay to play the field, as long as we play safe. What a dangerous message for any of us to embrace! We must remind ourselves and our children that there is no condom that can protect their minds from unwanted memories, and no condom can protect their hearts from the hurt of a cheap, one-night stand. We sell our children

Figure 2.13: Essentially, Kads Clothing is advocating "safe promiscuity."

short when we allow them to buy the notion that all they must do is "play safe" and "be careful."

While we're on the subject of premarital sex in advertising, let me mention one last item. From time to time an ad will emerge which uses double-entendre to reinforce this unbiblical view of sex. Consider this ad for St. Pauli Girl beer that reads, "You never forget your first Girl" (see figure 2.14). Which, of course, is a deliberate play on words—you never

Figure 2.14: St. Pauli Girl assumes everyone will have sex with more than one girl.

forget the first taste of a St. Pauli Girl beer, just like you never forget your first sexual conquest. Furthermore, supposedly it goes without saying, all men will have sex with several girls. That's a fact of life— or is it? If it's not on target, who will inform young eyes that these ad messages miss the mark?

Many more examples could be used to demonstrate the current trend of sexual themes in advertising. Admittedly, by the time you read this book, many of my examples will no longer be current. However, as long as the hearts of men are wicked, and as long as we allow wicked men to create and parade these images before our eyes (every time we buy one of these products, we are "voting" and paying for their livelihood), we can expect more of the same—if not worse—in the days ahead.

For the sake of balance, permit me to discuss one additional ad. This advertisement by the Coty company features a handsome man and attractive woman (see figure 2.15). The slogan is, "I love only one man, I wear only one fragrance."

Frankly, I don't personally care how many fragrances clutter our countertops. There is something refreshing, however, about the perspective this ad presents on romance: *one* man with *one* woman, *with* clothes! In contrast to those Calvin Klein ads, this advertisement is a breath of fresh air. Part of our goal is to help our children understand that we're not against sex; we're against *bad* sex. And thankfully, as we attempt to help them see that point, there are some ads (though not as many as I'd like to see) that handle romance responsibly.

You may recall in the first chapter I stated that there was a time in American history when the primary centers of learning were limited to the school, the church, and the home. Today, however, a fourth center of learning has emerged—the voices of popular media and entertainment. In this chapter I've gone to some length to illustrate two primary concerns about the powerful and persuasive voice of advertising: (1) ads that work to undermine self-esteem by providing our daughters with a false standard of beauty; and (2) ads that sell our children a warped understanding of human sexuality.

I trust this overview enables you to better understand the challenge advertising can present to a generation of children at risk. At the same time, having studied this material, you may be feeling angered, overwhelmed, even despairing. Hang in there! As we'll learn in a

I love only one man.
I wear only one fragrance.

Figure 2.15: Coty offers a more balanced picture of romance.

subsequent chapter, by sharpening our skills of discernment we *can* equip our children so that they won't become prey for the pied piper of Madison Avenue.

3

FLIRTING WITH DELILAH

*T*he telephone rang; it was one of those calls parents dread. From several states away daughter Missy was calling with the painful news of her divorce. Her mom was the first to reach the phone. Fighting back the tears, she fumbled to offer words of comfort for her daughter. After hanging up, she sought the support of her husband. "Honey, I've got to talk with you—something has happened to Missy."

Dad, with his eyes glued to the television, managed to mumble, "You'll have to wait until the commercial break," and with a wave of his hand he dismissed her.

Dumbfounded, she replied, "But this is very serious, dear. We need to talk *now*."

Anger filled his voice as he shot back, "Now you listen to me, whatever it is, it *can* wait until the *commercials!*"

This woman reached out for the supporting hand of her spouse in a moment of grave need. What did she receive? The mute button of her husband's remote control zapping her crisis.

I know some readers may find this true story tough to believe. After all, what companion could be so callous? How could anyone allow television to take priority at a time like that? On the other hand, perhaps this encounter is all too familiar. You've watched the tube invade your home over the years; you even detect its impact on the youngest children.

A homemaker from Wisconsin wrote me with this observation: "I am a mother of three boys, ages seven, four, and two. Lately, my husband and I have noticed that the more TV they watch, the more uncommunicative they become. All they want to do is watch television. When they view a lot, they become cranky and unwilling to do what's asked of them."

Then there's the letter from a woman whose husband failed to support her efforts to protect their youngsters from television's assault: "My husband is a good man but works too much and is 'spent' when at home. He wants to relax—that means TV hour after hour. I often find myself standing alone in my vigil to keep excessive violence, foul language, and explicit sex out of our home."

Reflecting upon these three situations, I have to wonder what went wrong. After all, the introduction of television in 1939 (some readers may remember a time when TV was commonly referred to as "the Philco") was lauded by many as one of the most promising technological advances of mankind. Its very name (loosely translated, "to see far") implied that TV coverage would expand the frontiers of our conversation; through its window we could see and share remote parts of the world previously inaccessible to us. The birth of this "electronic baby" marked the beginning of the information age.

THE FOUR TENETS OF THE COUCH POTATO

Not everyone embraced this new, one-eyed wonder with open arms. During the late forties, Dr. Edward J. Carnell, a professor at Fuller Theological Seminary, penned the book *TV: Servant or Master?* With a prophetic flair, he observed that television could easily become the master of our homes. He was among the few who predicted that this communications breakthrough also had the power to shred the channels of dialogue between husband and wife, father and son, mother and daughter.

For better or worse, the way our world communicates has been revolutionized by TV, and it's here to stay. Whether it will be our servant or master will be determined by us. How about you? Do you want to regain control of "the Philco"? Then sharpening the skills of discernment as it pertains to our TV diet is the first step, and the focal point of this chapter. If we are to be successful in our efforts to refocus the role of television in the home, we must address four commonly held "beliefs" that ultimately blur the vision of a discerning spirit and cripple the critical thinking process.

1. Television has *always* played a dominant part in our culture. Come to think of it, everyone we've ever known has at least one. Television must obviously be a staple of life, a necessity.

2. TV tells it like it *really* is. In other words, television accurately mirrors the world we live in and is trustworthy. Programmers who design what we watch share our values.

3. The alleged decline in broadcast standards is a myth.

4. Watching hours of television day after day is normal behavior. How could anyone seriously question our stewardship of time? After all, Americans have a right to continuous entertainment. There's no need to regulate its usage.

Frequently I've observed that these four beliefs are used to create a wall of denial around folks with skewed viewing habits. Left unchallenged, these beliefs pave the way for the television to become master rather than servant. And frankly, I fear this modern plug-in drug has more of us addicted and in a state of denial than at any other time in history.

> **"I fear this modern plug-in drug (TV) has more of us addicted and in a state of denial than at any other time in history."**

If you don't agree or appreciate this assessment, before changing the channel keep in mind that I still own a TV. I'm not proposing that we should rush to the city dump with our "boob tubes"—or stage "set smashing sessions" on the church parking lot (although you may elect to do that at some point). Rather, permit me a few moments to offer some perspective on the above four tenets of a couch potato.

The Two-TV Family

"Let me see the hands of you who have a television in your home." Whenever I ask a class of youngsters to do that, invariably someone lets out a resounding "Duh!" What they're really expressing is amazement that anyone could ask such a dumb question. Yes, contrary to the first belief—that television has *always* played a dominant part in our culture—there was a time, only about fifty years back, when television sets were scarce, even nonexistent.

It's interesting to watch the faces of fourth graders as I help them understand this fact of life. They wrongly assume that television, like God, has always been around. Inevitably someone in the class will ask, usually with a touch of astonishment in his voice, "What did people do for fun before TV?" I believe behind their bewilderment lies another question: How is it *possible* to have fun without it? Frankly, I don't blame them for their thinking. After all, our chatty electronic friend-in-the-box has become a regular family member, not to mention the primary focus of entertainment in most households.

I believe we take the presence of television in our homes too much for granted. We rarely bother to wonder what life *would* be like without it. Once, as a somewhat radical teenager who was wrestling with these thoughts, I came across the story of a man describing his first encounters with the tube, when the television era was still in its infancy. Since I was not old enough to have such memories, I found his first impressions fascinating. He writes:

> I can vividly remember the time some thirty years ago at about age six when I incurred my parents' wrath for sneaking into a bar. I had huddled in the back to catch a glimpse of the incomparable new invention—the television set, at that time a small round screen within a very big box—and the bar had the only set anyone knew about. Equally strong in my memory is the time, at about age ten, when my parents took me to one of their friend's house on a Friday night so I could see the Red Sox play the Yankees on television, an experience to me of such ecstasy and marvel I lay awake all night replaying the game in my mind.
>
> That first introduction to television and the sense of fascination, suspense, indeed almost a suspicion that one was approaching the edge of the supernatural, could only be found today in a pre-twentieth-century remote culture. The television set is no longer a novelty or luxury or wonder; it has become a standard piece in the furnishing of the American home (replacing the dining table as the center of the family) and is regarded as a foremost necessity.[1]

The days of sneaking out to a bar or going to a friend's house to catch a glimpse of television is a faded memory. In just fifty years, over 98 percent of the homes in America now own at least one television set.

(Interestingly, only 96 percent of the houses in America have an indoor toilet. This is the first time in our nation's history when we have more garbage coming into our homes than flowing out of them!)

No, contrary to the belief that television has always dominated our culture, it's only about fifty years old. For the sake of perspective, then, let's trace the rapid growth of the television industry. The sale of black-and-white television sets first took place in 1939 at an average price of six hundred dollars. By comparison, new cars were sold for only about one thousand dollars. Few purchased a TV due to the expensive price tag, not to mention there was virtually nothing on the airwaves! Television production was put to a halt once America entered World War II; engineers were put to work on radar development instead. Once the war ended, the race to mass-produce televisions went into full gear.

Commercial TV took off in 1946. Black-and-white screens were still the norm as four networks—ABC, CBS, NBC, and the DuMont TV network—developed a daily program schedule. Color television marked a major breakthrough, surpassed only by the creation of home video machines. Sony introduced the Betamax in February of 1976 which sold for $1,295 wholesale. By 1983, the average wholesale price of a VCR dropped to $470. Two years later it was $350. In 1986, there was a dramatic decrease in prices due to Japanese and Korean competition, with prices as low as $200—not much more than the cost of a typical repair.

One reason many of us wrongly assume that television has always been an intricate part of our society is the dominant role it now enjoys. No doubt television owes this elevated status to the expansion of TV-dependent devices: video players, laser discs, satellite dishes, Nintendo-type games, and cable. And it's only logical: the more options we have to make use of our television set, the more time we will likely spend sitting in its presence.

Take, for instance, our increased appetite for viewing movies at home. In 1980, less than two million households had a video player (commonly called a VCR). Only ten years later, more than sixty-two million homes owned a VCR—a 3,265 percent increase (see table 3.1 below for breakdowns).[2] With so many families now equipped with a video player, the sales of prerecorded videotapes to U.S. dealers, excluding public domain and "adult"-porno titles, experienced a dramatic increase.

In 1980, dealer sales were a meager three million units. By 1989, paralleling the growth of VCR sales, dealers met demand by purchasing

Table 3.1 Increase of Homes with VCRs		
Year	Homes with a VCR	Percent of increase from 1980
1980	1,850,000	
1984	15,000,000	716%
1987	45,800,000	2,376%
1989	62,259,600	3,265%

a total of two hundred million prerecorded videotapes—a 6,566 percent increase![3] You can bet that, along with the introduction of the video player, numerous families have expanded the number of hours they spend viewing TV. Next time you're at the video store, take a look at the folks standing in line at the check-out counter. Chances are you'll find many customers holding three tapes; that's six hours of watching the box!

Here's the punch line: The more time we spend focused on the tube, the more difficult it becomes for us to remember a time when TV viewing was the exception—not the norm, that indeed there *is* life without TV. I can't blame a child who believes that television "always was." He doesn't know any better. But you and I do. To regain control of the tube in our homes, the first step is to remember that television (and the myriad of TV-dependent devices) is a gift to those of us in this century, unknown by all others in ages past. We must not lose sight that this gift, if mismanaged, has the power to reduce us to a nation of "vidiots."[4]

Remote Controlled

The second belief (TV tells it like it *really* is) is simply untrue. Let me provide you with several reasons why. If you've ever played around with a home video camera, you'll identify with my first reason. During the Thanksgiving holidays in 1987, I had a torn Achilles tendon which meant I couldn't play in my family's annual Turkey Bowl backyard football game. Guess who was volunteered to video the game. Standing on the sidelines, camera in hand, I proceeded to capture the game on tape.

I soon discovered the power of my position as cameraman and narrator. What the rest of the family would ultimately watch depended on what *I* thought was important to film. Brother Steve is going deep for a long pass in the end zone—do I tape that? Or do I focus on my brother Tim, who's in a headlock with Uncle Chris back at the line of scrimmage?

Although this is a somewhat elementary example, it illustrates what I call "the directed eye." As you and I sit before the television set, we

---

"The more time we spend focused on the tube, the more difficult it becomes for us to remember a time when TV viewing was the exception—not the norm, that indeed there is life without TV."

---

voluntarily give over the control of our eyes to the producer of what we are watching. We will only see what he wants us to see. And depending upon the camera angle, what we *think* we are seeing may not be what *actually* took place. When we are watching television, our eyes are always directed to experience that which may or may not be true—true as defined by a cast of technicians, producers, and editors.

Author Kevin Perotta further illuminates the point: "The choice of subject matter, the way the subject will be dealt with, what will be shown and what will be excluded [framing], what will be treated as important and what ignored—these are decisions that the writer, director, cameraman, and producer have made. The program which results shows us life happening from their point of view."[5]

In some ways, it's a frightening thought to realize that when we watch television, we are seeing life happening through someone else's eyes. Perotta points out that "before the development of motion pictures around the turn of the century, no one ever saw anything *happening* through anyone else's eyes."[6] In other words, television allows us to "get inside" the mind of a lunatic, a rapist, a murderer, an adulterer. We, sitting in our chairs, can experience vicariously the feelings, sights, and emotions of these troubled individuals. There's a world of difference between a storyteller describing various encounters in the "first person," prompting ideas in the mind of the listener, and actually experiencing life in his or her shoes.

Another reason why television doesn't tell it like it is can be found in the limitations of the medium itself. Television can only bring us visuals and sound. Our senses of smell, taste, and touch are never utilized. When watching a commercial that pictures a hot, fresh cinnamon-nut loaf coming out of the oven, we can't smell it, we can't touch it, and, as much as we may want to, we can't actually judge for ourselves if it tastes any good.

Often, those who bring us television programming would like to make us think that something is real when in actuality it isn't. For example, virtually all studio sets are fake. Oh, they look real enough, but the city lights pictured behind Johnny Carson's desk on the "Tonight Show" aren't *real* city lights. The living room used by Bill Cosby on the "Cosby Show" isn't located in a real house. When a weatherman points to the weather map, guess what? In the more sophisticated studios he's actually pointing to a blank wall. The "map" is electronically superimposed.

A more dangerous example of TV's inaccurate portrayal of reality is found in its treatment of sex. On average, viewers will watch at least nine thousand scenes of suggested sexual intercourse during prime time annually;[7] 80 percent of these encounters are outside of marriage.[8] Think about it. When was the last time you saw someone on television involved in a sexual encounter outside of marriage contract a sexually transmitted disease (STD)? Personally, outside of an occasional special on AIDS, I can't recall a single instance. Out of fairness, if television is going to display people routinely involved in sex during the soap operas, evening soaps, or feature movies, it should also display the consequences of such activity. Instead, our eyes are directed to a false impression of reality. The lesson: we can sleep around with no harmful results.

There's one last example worth mentioning of the warped view of reality that television can create. In a special Public Broadcasting System television series called "The Public Mind," President Reagan's media director Michael Deaver confessed that public opinion about a potential candidate can be shaped through a mingling of fact and fiction. He observed, "Pictures can make stories out of nothing," and "It's not the *facts* of the story but the *coverage* that wins out"[9] (emphasis added). Candidates don't necessarily have to discuss facts or critical issues. Rather, if they are simply *pictured* as being sympathetic to the environment, the homeless, or whatever, the viewer is led to believe they'll do something about it.

Many more examples could be discussed to demonstrate the fact that television frequently does not portray a dependable picture of reality, including the way TV avoids picturing people praying, attending church, or reading the Bible.

To admit, then, that this "family member" is actually a chronic liar and an expert of illusion is a small, but vital step in our journey to becoming critical thinkers.

That's Entertainment?

The third belief of a couch potato is that the alleged decline in broadcast standards is a myth. Has television programming deteriorated with age?

Former Federal Communications Commission chairman Newton Minow once described television as "a procession of game shows, violence, formula comedies . . . more violence . . . Western bad men, private eyes . . . cartoons . . . and, endlessly, commercials."[10] He made these comments while addressing the annual convention of the National Association of Broadcasters. At one point in this penetrating speech, he referred to television as a "vast wasteland." The year: 1961. Television was only twenty years old and already a problem child!

Actually, any serious student of television standards could easily document TV's slide into the sewer. A few examples of this change will suffice. Remember Lucy Ricardo? Lucy shocked the world in 1952 when she announced on the "I Love Lucy" show, at a time when you couldn't say "pregnant" on the air, that she was having a baby. During this era, separate beds for *married* couples was the rule, and when filming bedroom scenes, full pajamas were a must!

"Search for Tomorrow," "General Hospital," "Dallas," "Dynasty," "Knots Landing," "L.A. Law"—before long the depiction of fornication, adultery, and even partial nudity was commonplace. Why? According to Dick Wolf, coproducer of "Miami Vice" and one who prides himself in pushing TV's sexual frontier, "It's always better to push than to be static and just have a chaste kiss on the cheek."[11] He went so far as to picture a passionate lovemaking scene intercut with the graphic murder of a prostitute—a sick merger of the emotional impact of sex and violence.

With regard to violent programs, in 1990 (thanks to the Fox Broadcasting network) horror movie "star" Freddy Krueger had his own violent-intensive weekly feature called "Freddy's Nightmares." One episode featured graphic acts of cannibalism. Other shows routinely included dismemberment, buckets of blood, and various explicit methods of torture I'd rather not detail. To be sure, television's declining broadcast standards as evidenced by shows such as these prompted, in part, President Bush to sign into law the TV Violence Act of 1990. The Act grants the television industry a three-year exemption from antitrust laws to permit discussion and the development of voluntary guidelines "designed to alleviate the negative impact of violence in telecast material."[12]

In spite of this call to reduce the negative impact of violence, as I write this page California lawmakers are considering lifting the ban on videocameras at executions—why? Pressure is building from the television industry to air these moments of actual death. We shouldn't be too surprised to see executions during prime time. Though repulsive, the exploration of televised death is a natural extension of the philosophy of Alfred Hitchcock. While studying his approach to filmmaking, I recall him explaining that his love of film was far more important to him than any other considerations of morality. As long as TV producers adhere to his philosophy, we can expect the picture of TV to worsen with time.

Actually, this undressing of our public virtue should come as no surprise in a free-market system. In order to attract larger audiences, the networks find themselves in a race to be racy. What complicates the picture is the competition from cable; cable is not regulated as tightly as broadcast television. This freedom allows cable to display virtually anything. If the networks are going to compete with cable, they assume pushing the lines of decency is the only way to keep ahead.

But at what cost? I believe each television episode that exploits sex, violence, and cheap thrills moves society further down the pathway of moral numbness.

Perhaps the best way to understand this is to remember the first time you rode a roller coaster. If you're like me, as you approached the first rise and sharp fall, your heart raced to the top of your throat while you held on for dear life. By the time you came to the grand finale—a straight drop from what seemed to be the height of a skyscraper—you had confessed all of your sins and were ready to die. But you didn't die. And after several more rides you became quite used to it. Space Mountain at Disney World offered new possibilities with its speeds of over sixty miles per hour—in total darkness! Having mastered that, the famous Loch Ness Monster at Busch Gardens, featuring an upside-down figure eight, appeared to be the final frontier.

> ## *"In order to attract larger audiences, the networks find themselves in a race to be racy."*

What once shocked our sensibilities has now become commonplace. In order to obtain the same level of thrill, we must subject our senses to something more exotic. Frankly, in the short fifty years of television, it appears we've become a nation of voyeurs.

Mark Twain once observed, "Man is the only blushing animal—and the only one that needs to." Thinking critically about the television we watch is hampered when we lose our ability to avert our eyes.

Stay with Us . . . We'll Be Right Back

The fourth commonly held belief of a TV consumer is that watching hours of television day after day is normal behavior. I can hear the voices of protest: "How could anyone seriously question our stewardship of time. After all, Americans have a right to continuous entertainment."

Let's assume that watching hour after hour of television is your right. Further, for the sake of argument, let's say that everything you watch is not packed with negative values. Several questions still persist. Like, how much viewing is too much? What else could or should you do with the time? Is this the best use of your time? Will you and I be accountable for the time we've wasted staring into the eye of that vast television wilderness?

Consider the story of John. John was an inmate on death row awaiting his turn in the chair. Chuck Colson, chairman of Prison Fellowship, tells of a time when he offered John a television set. John smiled gratefully and said, "Thanks, but no thanks. You can waste an awful lot of time with those things." Colson wondered, *Waste time—on death row?*[13]

So just how much time are we talking about, anyway? According to figures released by the Neilsen Television Index, Americans averaged slightly more than *seven hours a day* in 1988–1989, up from four hours, forty-five minutes daily in 1950–1951 (see details below).

Average television hours watched per day from 1950 to 1989

Numbers have always interested me, especially these numbers. Watch what happens when we multiply less than half the national average of daily viewing (i.e., three hours per day) to calculate our lifetime TV viewing.

         3   Hours per day watching TV (this represents half the national average)
    x 7   Days per week
     21   Hours spent watching TV per week

     21   Hours per week in front of the tube
    x 50   Weeks per year (assume you're on vacation for two weeks without a TV!)
    1,050   Hours spent watching TV per year—at half the national average!

For the sake of this mathematical analysis, we'll limit our focus to the sixty-year period between ages five and sixty-five. I do this because we all know that viewing TV under age five is bad for early childhood development, and most of us have to stop watching at age sixty-five because our eyes have dried up and fallen out!

1,050	Hours spent watching TV per year
x 60	Years of viewing TV (between ages five and sixty-five)
63,000	Hours watching the babbling box by age sixty-five at *half* the national average

Can you believe it? By watching television only three hours per day, by the time we retire we'll have clocked 63,000 hours. Ugh! Admittedly, watching 63,000 hours of television is a lot, but my mathematical inquisitiveness wants to know exactly how much that equals in practical terms.

63,000.00	Cumulative hours viewing TV by age sixty-five
÷ 8,760.00	Total # hours available per year (24 hours/day x 365 days/year)
7.19	Number of *years* watching television

Did you catch that? If you view 63,000 hours of TV by age sixty-five, that is the equivalent of watching more than seven years of television around the clock. What else could you do with 10 percent of your life? How about going to college two more times? Thoughts of pursuing a second career? How about all of those projects you never had time for? Not to mention the time you didn't have for your children or spouse.

Having worked through this math, do me a favor. Before turning the television back on, ask yourself some of these important questions about stewardship and time management. Evaluate the return upon your investment of time in front of the tube. What dividends does it pay? Are you a better person? Imagine what you'd be like if you spent seven years of your life reading the Bible instead of sailing on the Love Boat.

In 1991, the Texas Instruments company ran a two-page ad in several publications with this headline: "A third grader spends an average of 900 hours a year in class. And 1,170 hours watching television." It pictured a young boy eating a bowl of popcorn. His glazed eyes were glued to the set, held spellbound in a television-produced stupor. The thought struck me that anyone who spends 1,170 hours a year doing any one activity must really enjoy what they're doing or be addicted to it. What about you?

Coming to terms with the fact that watching hours of television day after day is both abnormal and unhealthy is vital if we who are video veggies are to regain our vision.

DON'T TOUCH THAT DIAL

I'm reminded of a peculiar habit of my great-grandmother. Although I was only a little boy while she was alive, I recall two things. First, this godly woman would read her Bible with a magnifying glass, sitting in "Big Grandma's chair" for hours at a time. Second, because she was ninety-one years old, she didn't fully understand what a television set was. Whenever one of us would turn it on while she was reading, she'd immediately ask for a blanket to cover herself because she thought the people on TV could see *us* sitting in the living room! How's that for a switch—being "decent" for the television!

Recognizing that the ideals of decency, modesty, restraint, and discretion were routinely discarded by television producers, Italian bishop Gilberto Baroni asked the faithful during the season of Lent in 1987 to consider switching off their televisions for forty days. He wrote, "Dearly beloved, the forty-day fast can also be done by renouncing your television. We must know how to react to this epidemic of video dependence, this mania to want to see everything. The television blares for hours and hours in all houses with no respect for silence, for tranquility."[14] His creative suggestion sparked controversy around the world.

I remember that this imaginative suggestion prompted me to raise a series of questions about my viewing habits and about television shows in general. I wondered, *Would Jesus watch "Wheel of Fortune?" Would Jesus watch TV at all? What would He watch?* These questions ultimately led me to rewrite Psalm 23 with soap operas in mind.

> TV is my shepherd, I shall not want.
> It alloweth me to lie down in my reclining chair.
> It leadeth me beside Luke and Laura.
> It entertaineth my soul.
> It leadeth me thru many a dull afternoon—
>   for the advertisers' sake.
> Yea, though I walk thru the valley
>   of the shadow of boredom, I will fear no evil.
> For thou, TV, art with me.
> Thy game shows and soap operas, they comfort me.
> Thou preparest a daily program schedule before me,
>   in the presence of my *TV Guide.*
> Thou anointest my head with a sea of sensuality,

my discretion runneth out.
Surely, good times and mindlessness will follow me
    (and "All My Children") all of the "Days of Our Lives."
And we will dwell in the presence
    of thy "Guiding Light" forever!

MAN OF STEEL

Do you remember the story of Samson? Samson was the strongest man in the Bible—a man of steel, as it were. As a youngster Samson killed a lion with his bare hands; he was that powerful. Later, he singlehandedly caught three hundred foxes and tied their tails together in pairs. His

> *"Recognizing that the ideals of decency, modesty, restraint, and discretion were routinely discarded by television producers, Italian bishop Gilberto Baroni asked the faithful during the season of Lent in 1987 to consider switching off their televisions for forty days."*

great strength was never more evident than the time he was attacked by a thousand Philistines; that's one thousand men against one. With God's help, Samson killed the entire lot; his only weapon was a jawbone from a donkey.

What does this have to do with TV and discernment? Having recently studied the story of Samson, I believe there's a fundamental principle we can learn about television from his life. To understand this concept, a few historical details are needed. First, Israel had been persecuted by the Philistines for forty years. In His mercy, God decided to provide one who would free them from their oppression since they had no king. Second, like Jesus' birth, Samson's was foretold by an angel, and his parents were given special instructions on how to raise him.

Third, God created Samson to do a job—to be the judge of Israel. For about twenty years, he fulfilled this high calling.

But there was a complication. Samson had a weakness for women. In Judges 16, we find this man of steel spending the night with a prostitute. His next exploit was a Philistine woman named Delilah. You probably know how the story goes—Delilah begged Samson to reveal the source of his great strength. After stringing her along with a series of bogus answers, he finally gave in to her persistent pleas. "A razor has never come on my head, for I have been a Nazirite to God from my mother's womb. If I am shaved, then my strength will leave me and I shall become weak and be like any other man" (Judges 16:17).

While Samson was asleep on her lap, Delilah had his hair shaved off and called for the Philistine lords to attack him. As he had predicted, Samson's strength left him, and he became like any other man. It's interesting to notice what the Philistines did immediately after seizing Samson—they gouged out his eyes.

What was the judge of Israel doing sleeping with the enemy? Didn't he realize he was flirting with fire? Yes, having his eyes wrenched from their sockets must have been an incredibly painful punishment. But I believe Samson suffered a greater nightmare than the darkness. The loss of his physical eyes would forever symbolize how he lost sight of his spiritual calling. Somewhere along the line, Samson—who should have known better—thought he could flirt with Delilah, could even embrace and confide in her, without any negative consequences.

Herein lies the principle for our discussion of TV. I believe Christians in the twentieth century have developed a deep love affair with their televisions. Blinded by the light of the tube, many have lost sight of their higher calling and have doomed themselves to sitting as prisoners of this week's program guide. Before dismissing this analogy out of hand, look at the parallels. Like Samson, we've been chosen for a high calling—in our case, it's to be salt and light to a hell-bound world. God provided Samson and you and me with extraordinary resources to accomplish this mission. Unfortunately, much like the man of steel, we've become too casual and comfortable with something that has the ability to destroy us. We even plan our lives (when we eat and sleep) around its program schedule. Television has become our master.

Samson flirted with Delilah and was ruined. A discerning spirit can equip us with the tools to avoid being seduced by the temptress of television.

"I believe Christians in the twentieth century have developed a deep love affair with their televisions. Blinded by the light of the tube, many have lost sight of their higher calling and have doomed themselves to sitting as prisoners of this week's program guide."

Tired of this dance with our modern-day Delilah? Don't lose heart! In a few pages we'll examine how to unglue ourselves—and our families—from the tube.

4

THE DECADE THE MUSIC DIED

*D*_{ear Bob,}

What did you do? Forget the other 'o' in your first name? I think your opinions suck and I'd like to meet you in person just so I could tell you off. I think your comment on KISS was totally off. KISS is not at all anti-Christian. I've heard all their tapes and not one I find offensive, and neither does my mother. I'm a Catholic, I go to a Catholic school so I'm sure I'd know an anti-Christ song if I found one. So why don't you get your head out of your pompous yuppie butt and listen to the music you are talking about.

⩲   ⩲   ⩲

This young teen wrote to me from Wisconsin in response to my "High Voltage" column on music and media in Focus on the Family's *Breakaway* magazine. Guess you can't please everyone. Oh, I might mention that one of his buddies also tucked in a letter calling me a "biased, simple-minded retard." This guy signed his letter "Sincerely, from an active Christian . . . I love God. I love hard rock." Over the years I've received thousands of letters from young fans, both nonbelievers and Christians. Many who have written sound as if they were willing to lay down their lives and die to prevent their favorite band from being criticized.

Yes, helping teens "learn to discern" appropriate music choices certainly has its challenges! Nevertheless, we have no option but to press on. Here's why. Pro-family leaders like Dr. James Dobson have warned us that the moral structure of a nation can be changed within just one generation. In my estimation, the powerful voices of the American youth culture that we're studying—advertising, television, and music—form one of the primary battlegrounds of this civil war of values. And, although the moderates and conservatives have made a number of significant public policy advances during the eighties and nineties (especially in terms of the presidency and Supreme Court), I believe we have nearly lost the youth entertainment cultural battle to the liberal camp.

SLIDING INTO THE SEWER

The following letters exemplify the pervasiveness of our deteriorating entertainment culture. This first letter was sent to me by a father in Maryland:

> Your recent newsletter emphasizing the lyrics of 2 Live Crew has prompted me to write. The question of effect upon our young people was brought home to me in a powerful way yesterday when my daughter relayed the following. Her story was confirmed by her brother. While riding the school bus home from school a boy began to recite some explicit rap lyrics. He then turned to my daughter, grabbed his crotch, and thrust himself at her while repeating lyrics similar to those you quoted in your newsletter.
>
> He then "invited" my daughter to his house to get "busted" [a street slang term used to describe taking one's virginity]. Maybe this is common everyday action today. But I don't remember classmates doing those things in the early sixties when I was a *second-grader!* I think times have changed, and it is evident that trash lyrics are affecting our youth. If this is the new second-grade action, what's left for those troubling teenage years?

Writing from Sioux Falls, South Dakota, Dawn shared her experience:

> I teach sixth grade and have done so for nine years. In May of this year [1990] we took our fifth and sixth graders on a field trip that required a two hour bus ride. Some of our students brought tape players and headsets to listen to on the long ride. During the trip, one of my students let me listen to a tape by the rap group N.W.A I was so disgusted with what I heard. And these were good kids from good homes! I asked more questions and was appalled to learn that their parents didn't care that they listened to this stuff. Then I found out that Mom and Dad really hadn't heard this tape! I can't tell you how many parents don't even know what their early adolescents are listening to.

Child psychologist Dr. David Elkind has observed that "one of the most underestimated influences on young people today is the music industry."[1] Why? Because, like the story of Rip Van Winkle cited earlier, we've been on an extended nap, ignoring the drastic changes that have been taking place directly under our noses. We've listened far too long to the "experts" who regularly assure us: (1) There's really nothing to be alarmed about in popular music. Things are the same today as when

> *"In my estimation, the powerful voices of the American youth culture that we're studying—advertising, television, and music—form one of the primary battlegrounds of this civil war of values."*

Elvis first shook the nation with his pelvis. (2) Children are not aware of the excesses in the music business (after all, they don't listen to the words—they just like the beat). (3) Music is only music, so it can't possibly have a negative influence on the listener—no matter what their age, no matter how deviant the message.

Are these assertions true?

In the pages that follow, I'll provide you with evidence that demonstrate things are *not* the same today as they were when Elvis sang "You Ain't Nothin' But a Hound Dog"; kids *are* plugged into their music in a very personal way; and that music *has* the power to influence the human spirit for good or for evil. I might add that many journalists contribute to the widespread social disease of ignorance by hiding this documentation from public scrutiny, opting to hide behind the smoke screen of alleged "free speech" rights. (I'll touch on that issue in chapter 9.)

Before we proceed, I need to clear the air on several key matters. First, our study is not intended to be a comprehensive analysis of the negative aspects of popular music. Entire books have been dedicated to that endeavor, such as Tipper Gore's *Raising PG Kids in an X-Rated Society* (Nashville, TN: Abingdon Press, 1987). For the purposes of this chapter, I will use six primary "mile markers" that chronicle the record industry's race to be raunchy during the second half of the eighties into the decade of the nineties. Keep in mind, the examples I'll be including are exactly that—examples. The moment this book is printed, my examples will drift further into history. However, any number of current events could be placed in the text.

Secondly, those who have heard me speak know that I am not an advocate of "hit lists." One mother approached me after a seminar and asked me to simply list the "bad guys" so she could guard against them. I had to explain that I don't provide hit lists. Why? For one reason, such lists are outdated faster than they could be written. More importantly, hit lists are counterproductive to the process of teaching and instilling discernment. As we'll see in the next chapter, learning to discern enables us to dispense with those lists of offenders.

There's one last matter I need to clarify. I am a musician who plays guitar, piano, and drums. I love and enjoy a wide spectrum of music. Based on more than a decade of serious study, I do not believe all secular music contains antisocial, deviant, or ungodly messages. There are many artists who exhibit positive, thought-provoking ideas in song. And contrary to several other speakers and authors that I've studied, I don't have an ax to grind about a particular musical style, backward masking (the dubious practice of playing records in reverse to uncover some hidden, evil message), or alleged "demon beats." My concern is primarily with the lyrical content by popular artists and the increasingly degrading, exploitive trend that has emerged in recent times. All styles of music—whether country and western, pop, folk, or rock—can, and often are, manipulated for the deviant purposes of the musicians who create them. Likewise, these same forms of music can be used to create songs that elevate the human spirit.

Having said that, let me recommend that you fasten your seat belt as we take what is sure to be a bumpy ride into the headphones of the younger generation.

STRETCHING THE LIMITS

Although not the purpose of this book, it would be an easy task documenting the fact that crude lyrical content and explicit album art were prolific within the pop music culture prior to 1985. During the late seventies and early eighties, all fingers pointed to hard rock and heavy metal music—two styles that became synonymous with degenerate ideas. The long list of bands who dwelt on the morbid side of life included folks like AC/DC, Led Zeppelin, Judas Priest, KISS, Motley Crüe, and Slayer.

"Based on more than a decade of serious study, I do not believe all secular music contains antisocial, deviant, or ungodly messages. There are many artists who exhibit positive, thought-provoking ideas in song."

But in the latter part of the eighties, turntables took a turn for the worse.

The emergence of "alternative" and rap musical styles expanded the frontier of depraved ideas. These idioms offered powerful communication possibilities to the "little guy"—to aspiring musicians who didn't have access to the mainstream pop music industry, who instead created music with home recording gear and a minimum of special effects. For example, just about any kid with an imagination and a beat (produced by either a drum or a mouth-generated sound effect) could rap. Holding a tune and skillful musicianship weren't prerequisites. Likewise, by definition, alternative music was a less refined, raw style that didn't require expensive industry polish. It avoided the trappings of a mass-appeal recording project and targeted a smaller, "underground" segment of the marketplace.

Yet, to be recognized in a morally numb youth culture, many alternative musicians worked overtime to shock the already dazed senses of teens. One example will suffice. A record low of sexual exploitation was set in 1985 by The Dead Kennedys, a Los Angeles-based punk-rock act, with the release of *Frankenchrist*. Folded inside of each record cover was a hard-core pornographic poster entitled "Penis Landscape," featuring more than a dozen close-ups of male/female copulation. The album, with the enclosed poster, was sold to children regardless of age. Lead singer Eric Boucher (a.k.a. Jello Biafra) dismissed their inexcusable pandering, asserting, "There is a label reading, 'The inside foldout to this record cover is a work of art by H. R. Giger that some people may find shocking, repulsive or offensive. Life can sometimes be that way.'"[2]

One mother in California disagreed that "life had to be that way" and took the band to court. Why? Apparently, someone gave her young preadolescent boy this album as a birthday present, forever robbing him of his youthful innocence. She believed that her family, as well as families around the country, should be protected from this flagrant violation of obscenity law. Much to her amazement, the judge and jury did not agree that their poster would be harmful to minors. She lost the case.

With all due respect to the legal system, it staggers the mind that those who are committed to administering justice are sometimes incapable of applying a touch of common sense. On one hand, a court of law determines that the "Penis Landscape" poster is suitable viewing for children. On the other hand, there's *Playboy* magazine. Always looking for a "free speech" persecution angle to exploit, *Playboy* reported on the trial in a special news feature entitled, "Dead Liberties." However, when *Playboy* reprinted the poster as part of their story they blacked out all of the explicit parts! (Funny, aren't they the ones who rant about censorship?) I see. The poster is far too explicit for a pornographic, men's magazine but okay to sell to little children. To the best of my knowledge, when reporting on this trial, not one newspaper, not one magazine, nor any news program displayed the "harmless" poster in question. Instead, shortly after the trial, when I debated Jello Biafra on the nationally syndicated Michael Jackson radio program (no relationship to the musician by the same name), neither the host or Biafra would attempt to describe the poster in question. Thanks to the keepers of the media, the "porning" of young minds is one of America's best kept dirty secrets.

Some argue that the Dead Kennedys were a small, insignificant band with a limited following, thus the impact of this trial upon the culture was negligible. I maintain many cultural battles are fought at this level. You can be sure that the watchful eyes of music industry executives and retailers followed the legal proceedings of this case. Yes, another line of decency was crossed and left in the dust, paving the way for maladjusted bands with attitude problems to step into the limelight. Guns N' Roses is such a band.

GLORIFICATION OF UGLINESS

Guns N' Roses is noted for basically two things: deplorable attitudes about women and excessive substance abuse. These role models for a generation of impressionable fans seem to thrive on the controversy they generate and rumors which surround them. Their fondness for partying is well documented. Take, for example, this news coverage of one of their after-concert parties:

> According to several of the lucky invitees, the scene on the Troub's [Troubadour] balcony was straight out of Fellini, with naked groupies making out with each other on the tables. That's not really out of the ordinary for these kings of the debauched, but perhaps the highlight of the orgy was. Apparently, Mr. Rose found himself cheek to cheek (his upper, her lower) with one of the top-heavy Guns fans and proceeded to do what is now called "the Pee-wee bop" in front of the other guests (including members of his family), who held their amazement in check like the good, jaded Hollywoodians they are.[3]

And for lead guitarist, Slash, alcohol consumption was a way of life:

> I drank up to a half gallon of Vodka a day—easy. I got to the point where I was drinking so much, I would have the shakes so bad . . . the next morning, I would have to drink a fairly tall, stiff Vodka and cranberry just so I could drive.[4]

Bursting on the music scene virtually out of nowhere, their first album, *Appetite for Destruction,* was released in 1987 and sold more than twelve million copies; that's enough for virtually half of all the teens in America to own a copy. The original album cover art (see figure 4.1) featured an illustration in which a girl had apparently been raped. One of the T-shirts they sold featured

Figure 4.1: The original cover for Guns N' Roses album featured a rape scene (black out added).

this "rape scene" (see figure 4.2). You'll notice their slogan: "Guns N' Roses was here." The first time I spotted this tee was at the Dallas airport on the back of a boy that couldn't have been more than twelve years of age—traveling with

Figure 4.2: Guns N' Roses T-shirt for teens (black out added).

his mother! To get her attention, I felt like grabbing that mother by her shirt collar. I wanted to shout: "Hey, Mom! Do you see what your son is wearing? He's a walking ad for rape."

Lyrically, this debut from GNR was a celebration of their penchant for drinking, drugs, sex, and self-destruction. In "Nightrain" their love of barley and hops couldn't be more clear:

> Wake up late
> honey put on your clothes. Take your credit card
> to the liquor store. That's one for you and two for me
> by tonight I'll be
> Loaded like a freight train
> Flyin' like an aeroplane. Feelin' like a space brain . . .
> I'm on the nightrain
> Bottoms up
> I'm on the nightrain . . . ready to crash and burn
> I never learn . . . I love that stuff
> I'm on the nightrain
> I can never get enough.

"It's So Easy" continues their deplorable attitudes toward women:

> Why don't you just
> F—k off
> Ya get nothin' for nothin' If that's what ya do
> Turn around bitch I got a use for you
> Besides you ain't got nothin' better to do
> And I'm bored.

To be redundant, bands with an attitude problem have predated Guns N' Roses. What makes these perpetrators especially influential in the reshaping of our popular culture is the vast volume of records sold—twelve million on their debut—containing their warped ideology. And with the advent of portable tape players and headsets, Guns N' Roses have the power to whisper—no, shout—their morally bankrupt ideas directly into the heads of millions of teenagers.

A BAD RAP

While Guns N' Roses were rocking sold-out concert halls with their brand of derisive attitudes, 2 Live Crew rapped their way into legal history. The original king of obscene rappers, the Crew's release of their *Move Something* album [1985] generated a small wave of criticism. But in the fall of 1989, they managed to flood the nation's streets with their dirt-filled lyrics on *As Nasty As They Wanna Be* (see figure 4.3). One reason for the widespread interest in this record stemmed from a "clean" version of "Me So Horny" which rapidly became a top-forty hit tune on pop radio. And, as any record retailer can vouch, radio air play is the best formula to bolster sales.

In my estimation, prior to the release of *Nasty,* there had never been an album released in American history with

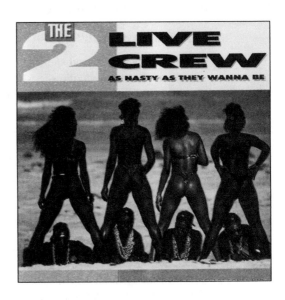

Figure 4.3: 2 Live Crew sold more than 1.6 million copies of this obscene album.

the degree of sexually degrading lyrical content as this. In my capacity as the youth culture specialist for Focus on the Family, I and my staff transcribed this double record set and found that the album included:

- 87 descriptions of oral sex
- 117 explicit references to male and female genitalia
- 226 uses of the "F"-word
- 163 uses of *bitch* when referring to women
- 81 uses of the vulgarity *sh _ _*
- 42 uses of *ass*

Among this garbage heap of lyrical imagery, the band added a reference to incest, several instances of group sex, and over a dozen illustrations of violent sexual acts.

Consider these two partial transcriptions from *As Nasty As They Wanna Be*. Keep in mind, these explicit lyrics were—and in many areas of the country, still are—sold to children regardless of age. I apologize for the explicit nature of these passages.

"Bad Ass Bitch"

My d _ _ k was hard and she was hot like a heater.
By the looks of her mouth, she was a d _ _ k eater.
I said you raggedy bitch don't play dumb.
Put my d _ _ k in your mouth
    and make this motherf _ _ker cum.
Ya! Yo! This bitch was on . . . Bad ass bitch.

"D _ _ k Almighty"

D _ _ k almighty's of no surprise.
It'll f _ _ k all the bitches, all shapes and size.
She'll climb a mountain, even run the block.
Just to kiss the head of this big black c _ _ k [slang for
    the male genital organ].
He'll tear the p _ _ sy [slang for the female genital
    organ] open, 'cause it's satisfaction.
The bitch won't leave, it's fatal attraction . . .
We're f _ _ king the bitch that's tight inside.
That d _ _ k has got a spell on you . . .
That d _ _ k almighty, d _ _ k almighty.

With the aforementioned lyrical analysis in mind, consider the mathematical aspect of repetition. When a child, the primary consumer of this album, listens to the record only ten times, he would be assaulted with 1,117 explicit descriptions of male and female genitalia while hearing 870 depictions of oral sex. Recognizing the implications of this, I

"When a child, the primary consumer of this album (As Nasty As They Wanna Be), listens to the record only ten times, he would be assaulted with 1,117 explicit descriptions of male and female genitalia while hearing 870 depictions of oral sex."

---

made the decision to launch an educational campaign, *after* the album had sold more than 1.4 million copies on its own. I say that because we were frequently accused of contributing to the promotion of their album by making an issue of it. This was simply not the case. As of this printing, the *Nasty* album still did not reach two million units sold, even with all of the national media attention it received.

On June 6, 1990, U.S. Federal District Court Judge Jose A. Gonzalez determined that this album was legally obscene—the first time in American history that a record album was successfully prosecuted as obscenity. In this landmark ruling, Judge Gonzalez stated: "The First Amendment is one of our most sacred liberties," but that "obscene speech has *no* protection under the First Amendment."

Some members of the recording industry protested this decision on the grounds that the album carried an explicit lyrics warning label. Judge Gonzalez countered, "To be redundant, obscenity is not a protected form of speech under the U.S. Constitution, with or without voluntary labeling. *It is a crime* [emphasis his]. The people of Florida have made obscenity a crime. The law is not a smorgasbord where people are free to pick and choose which laws they will obey and which they will reject." He underlined, "The First Amendment's guaranty is not absolute. Although the amendment is unconditional on its face, the fact that there were accepted state limits on speech at the time it was ratified indicates that the 'phrasing of the First Amendment was not intended to protect every utterance' (Roth, 354 U.S. at 483)."

John Leo, senior writer for *U.S. News and World Report,* pointed out the difference between a few vulgar words and the level of degradation of women rife in popular culture, calling 2 Live Crew "a pesky new pollutant." Commentator George Will in *Newsweek,* while attempting to characterize the cultural climate in America, coined the phrase "slide into the sewer."

But these writers, like me, are white and apparently don't understand the humor of the black community, or so lead singer Luther Campbell would have the public believe. According to Campbell, our concern about his exploitive lyrical content is racially motivated and demonstrates a misunderstanding of the black cultural experience. Furthermore, his music is supposed to be "comedy." In a *Los Angeles Times* editorial, Campbell says, "If anyone can't see that the 2 Live Crew is a comedy group, then I feel sorry for them. . . . 2 Live Crew's music—and lyrics—is nothing but a group of fellas bragging." Seeking sympathy, he wonders, "Why condemn me—a black artist and entrepreneur—for my particular brand of adult entertainment?"[5]

Is Campbell correct when he announces that he and his band represent the way black Americans communicate? Have we white folks just missed the "humor" of Campbell's brand of comedy? Dr. Benjamin Hooks of the National Association for the Advancement of Colored People (NAACP) protested Campbell's role as self-appointed spokesman for the black community. In a press release Dr. Hooks stated, "Our cultural experience does not include debasing our women, the glorification of violence, the promotion of deviant sexual behavior, or the tearing into shreds our cherished mores and standards of behavior."[6] (On a personal note, I've said it before, but let me go on record that I am as concerned about the sexual exploitation of little children—whether black, Hispanic, oriental, or any other culture—as I am concerned about white youth. 2 Live Crew's pornographic lyrics have *nothing* to do with race.)

While Luther Campbell was on television defending his obscene album, describing it as an African-American art form, the phone lines at the NAACP lit up. This prompted Dr. Hooks to emphatically state: "We are particularly offended by their efforts to wrap the mantle of the black cultural experience around their performances by saying this is the way it is in the black community, and that they are authentic purveyors of our heritage."[7]

During the heat of the media battle over explicit lyrics, Jason Berman, president of the Recording Association of America, went on record in defense of 2 Live Crew. In a *Billboard* editorial, he stated that *Nasty* was not hard-core pornography. If Berman does not think that an album which has been declared legally obscene by a U.S. Federal District Court is hard-core porn, then what is? Where does Berman draw the line? Essentially, he has given musicians a permission slip to be as socially irresponsible "as they wanna be." Yes, we are in a civil war of values. You cannot count on business leaders like Jason Berman to fight for the best interests of your children. Kids are consumer units. Maximizing profits, no matter how degrading the product, is Berman's and 2 Live Crew's bottom line.

MAINSTREAM MISOGYNY

America's slide into the sewer continues with a fourth example. Only a handful of artists ever record an album that sells more than five million copies. Such was the case in 1990 for white rap artist Vanilla Ice. *To the Extreme,* his debut album, sold in excess of seven million copies and was the number-one-selling record in America (see figure 4.4). He holds the dubious title of selling the *most* rap albums that feature a low regard for women, especially virgins.

Rather than belabor the point, I'll cite several brief examples. In the song "Ice Cold," he raps,

> Get excited and beg for more
> Get loose girl like a sex fiend, let's do it . . .
> Get hot and I ride like a sex machine.
>
> Be on the lookout in your vicinity,
> I'm robbin' virgins of their virginity.

"Stop That Train" was about groupie sex backstage, and "Life Is a Fantasy" was his dream fantasy with "beautiful girls rubbin' me down with some lotion . . . as we got busy [street slang for intimate sexual contact] . . . walked in the front door you startin' strippin' clothes . . . let me be your toy."

Vanilla Ice had an incredible made-for-MTV appeal, which allowed him to quickly amass a large following. Unfortunately, parents embraced his slick, cartoonish look and his smooth dance steps as harmless fun. It's also possible that because he was a white artist, white middle-class families welcomed his music with little or no scrutiny. This lack

Figure 4.4: More than 7 million youth bought the "soft porn" raps of Vanilla Ice.

of parental involvement allowed the Ice man's brand of misogyny to become the second largest selling rap album in history. Although he is not as lyrically vulgar as some of the other rappers we've discussed, his "soft porn" approach was an introduction to deviant sexual themes for a wide segment of the teen marketplace. His music likely opened the doorway to the world of lascivious rap as recorded by the likes of Too Short, Slick Rick, Eazy-E, and N.W.A.

UNLIKE A VIRGIN

As we chronicle the changes in the world of music entertainment, and given the predominant role that MTV plays in most homes, it would be a mistake to overlook the matter of explicit music videos in popular culture. Again, due to space limitations, I'd like to narrow our focus to a single event.

In the fall of 1990, Madonna released the video for her song "Justify My Love," a video filmed in Paris depicting her latest erotic sexual fantasies. That, in itself, should not have come as any surprise. After all, Madonna got her start in the entertainment business "acting" in a hard-core porno movie called "A Certain Sacrifice." This time Madonna, who loves to be on the edge of controversy, crossed a line. The folks at MTV couldn't justify airing her clip; it was *that* racy.[8]

What made this, the latest deviant product from the self-proclaimed "Boy Toy," so troubling? Within the span of a few minutes, the viewer would see explicit bisexual and group sex themes, coupled with voyeurism, sado-masochism, and some nudity. Attempting to defend this "artistic" effort, Madonna stated, "These fantasies and thoughts exist in every person. Why is it that people are willing to go to a movie and watch someone get blown to bits for no reason and nobody wants to see two girls kissing or two men snuggling?"[9]

Was MTV correct to pull the plug on Madonna's video? Should parents have the right to protest the sale of it to children at record stores? ABC decided to address the debate. Offering a few apologies and warnings of their own, ABC's "Nightline" aired the clip. Afterward, Forrest Sawyer and Madonna conversed about her latest controversy.

> SAWYER: You know how very hard it is for a parent to control the child having access to TV, and they sit there and they watch MTV all day long. If you were in that parent's position and it was your ten-year-old, would you not be worried about his seeing this kind of stuff?

> MADONNA: Personally, I wouldn't be worried about it. I think that if my video provokes an open discussion—maybe kids will go and ask their parents these questions. If it provokes an open discussion about sex with their parents, I think this is a really good thing.

> SAWYER: But, Madonna, you have to help me here. When a ten-year-old sees you chained to the bed or sees your boyfriend bound up, and another woman comes by while you're there, maybe *you* know that that's a fantasy, but a ten-year-old's going to get awfully confused here.

> MADONNA: Good. Then let them get confused and let them go ask their parents about it, and let their parents, you know, explain to them that it is a sexual fantasy.[10]

Music makers like Madonna believe there is no problem broadcasting explicit bisexual material across our airwaves, even for the consumption of children. And for those who believe that popular entertainment hasn't changed much in recent times, one thing is sure: a couple of hip wiggles from Elvis's highly controversial appearance on

Figure 4.5: Reprinted by permission: Tribune Media Services

the Ed Sullivan show is no match for Madonna's brazen video sexploitation (see figure 4.5).

A NEW HIGH BRINGS AMERICAN CULTURE TO A NEW LOW

It was business as usual when I got a call from a reporter. "Hi, Bob, Chuck Phillips from the *Los Angeles Times*. Guess you heard that N.W.A's new album *Niggaz4life* (see figure 4.6) just captured the number one spot on *Billboard*'s pop charts. I'm doing a story and wonder if you have any comments?" I knew it was bound to happen, but I was angered nonetheless. How could an album with an explicit lyrics warning label, with lyrics that rivaled the sexually degrading and violent themes of 2 Live Crew and the Geto Boys, enter the pop album chart at number two and jump to the top spot in only two weeks, without *any* radio air play? N.W.A received no

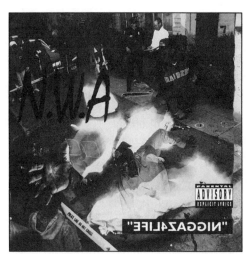

Figure 4.6: N. W. A sold a million copies of this obscene album.

radio support because every song on that record, if played over the airwaves, would violate the Federal Communications Commission broadcasting standards.

What was worse, *Niggaz4life* sold a million copies in only three weeks of its release. My mind raced for an explanation. Could it be that there are a million families whose parents just don't care what their children put into their impressionable minds? Or are there that many kids who have no parental supervision? In either case, the popular entertainment culture slipped to a new low. How bad could this album be if record stores in malls all across the country, even in middle-class suburban areas, were selling it to children? You be the judge.

Once again, let me apologize in advance for the graphic lyrical content of these tunes. There is no way for you to fully understand the assault upon the minds of children in this country until you see for yourself what is playing in the theater of their minds via their headphones. As you consider the evidence, keep in mind the partial transcription of these two songs was taken from the number one selling album in America on June 22, 1991.

"Findum, F _ _ kum and Flee"

Easily I'm approachin', there ain't no jokin',
When the p _ _ sy holes are open.
Ready to f _ _ k until my d _ _ k is raw,
Yo, the motherf _ _ kin' devil's son-in-law.
Peter, Peter, the p _ _sy eater.
No, it's the E, the motherf _ _ kin' p _ _ sy beater.
And I'm the quicker picker-upper, quick to pick up a bitch.
So come here, bitch, and
    lick up the, lick up the, lick up the d _ _ k . . .

"She Swallowed It"

This is a bitch that did the whole crew . . .
Because the dumb bitch licks out their assh _ _ _.
And they'll let ya videotape her.
And if ya got a gang of niggers
    the bitch'll let ya rape her.
She likes suckin' on d _ _ ks and lickin' up nut.
And they even take the broomstick up the butt.
Just to say that she did it with a rapper . . .

Other songs such as "One Less Bitch" and "To Kill a Hooker" are riddled with violence toward women. Those, my dear reader, are wretched lyrics to wade through. If you have difficulty digesting what you've just read through one time, imagine the damage experienced by young listeners with impressionable minds who play that album twice, ten, even thirty times, who may be listening to its deplorable message even now.

MIND GAMES

I was invited to be on the nationally syndicated "Good Morning America" television show to discuss the alarming state of the world of pop entertainment. I'll never forget the dialogue at one point in the conversation between host Mike Schneider and Jennifer Dargan, a black, premed student at Harvard University. Having quoted a few lines from "One Less Bitch" by N.W.A, Mike asked Jennifer:

[Harvard is] a school filled with a sense of renewed vigor now on so-called political correctness. . . . These lyrics seem to be lyrics that involve hate toward women, coercive sexual activity, rape, violence, yet you call yourself a fan.

JENNIFER explained: Well, I don't know if I would necessarily say that just because they talk about violence that they espouse violence towards women.

SCHNEIDER countered: Yet you wouldn't want to be referred to as a bitch.

DARGAN: I don't think that they're referring to me or anyone that I know when they—

SCHNEIDER: Well, they say "*all* women are bitches."[11]

This pre-med fan of N.W.A holds an indefensible position. I'm not attempting to slam Ms. Dargan; however, when someone attempts to justify misogyny, he or she has to resort to mind games and dodge ball. I expect more from a Harvard student and the educational community. Instead, many who should know better, whether fans or not, commit intellectual suicide, standing logic on its head in order to excuse exploitive lyrics.

Fortunately, a few black journalists stepped forward to condemn N.W.A's hate-filled rap. Janine McAdams, a writer for *Billboard*, refused to applaud N.W.A's enormous sales success. Instead, she believed this album took "misogyny to hateful extremes." In the final analysis, "If this kind of musical message is the wave of the future, then we are surely without hope."[12] And, writing for the *Miami Herald*, Leonard Pitts, Jr., asked, "Maybe I'm crazy, but am I the only one who thinks it obscene that this popular new genre was born out of the exploitation of a sick violence that has wrecked thousands of lives?" He adds, "I'm not saying gangsta rap causes this tragedy but that it legitimizes it."[13]

Much to my amazement, *Time* magazine took a break from their "anything goes" editorial position for a few minutes to side with conservatives: "Listening to a continual obscene litany about bitches, hos, and the things they want or are willing to do with the group's sex organs is an exercise in brutalization. It doesn't make N.W.A seem baaad, it makes them look awful."[14] Even musician Sinead O'Connor did an about-face. O'Connor had previously stood by N.W.A's right to advocate the murder of police in a tune called "F_ _ _ tha Police." When the target shifted to women, O'Connor went on record stating N.W.A's "attitudes have become increasingly dangerous. The way they deal with women in their songs is pathetic."[15]

I am pleased to report that there were a few bright spots on the retail level as well. K-Mart and Wal-Mart refused to carry the product. Likewise, the Kentucky-based, 140-store chain of Waxworks record stores would not stock *Niggaz4life*. President Terry Woodward had this to say of N.W.A's product, "I personally think it's a black eye on the whole industry. I'm not sure what that says about our consumer right now."[16] Nor am I.

IS IT ONLY ROCK 'N' ROLL?

If I've accomplished nothing more, I trust that the six examples I've just cited make this fact absolutely clear: what passes for musical entertainment today, on the multimillion-selling albums which kids are buying, is far more troubling than the worst examples one could subpoena from the fifties, sixties, or even the seventies. There is no room or time for continued denial. But can music actually influence a child's behavior? Read the following three accounts before jumping to any conclusions.

Seventeen-year-old Michael Billings pleaded guilty. Sixteen-year-old Bobby Titsworth pleaded guilty. Stephane Wartson, seventeen, and Robert Wartson, twenty, also pleaded guilty. Their crime? Kidnapping and gang raping two girls from Muskogee High School. The *Tulsa Tribune* reported that, while waiting for the school bus, one of the girls was dragged into a car. The other youngster was kidnapped that same morning as she stood in front of her high school. Both were taken to a house where they were repeatedly raped and beaten with a belt. (The girls were ninth and tenth graders.)

What makes this case particularly troubling is the fact that the boys played a rap song entitled "Gangster of Love" by the Geto Boys several times during the ordeal. District Attorney Drew Edmondson, who is handling the case, believes this music may have fueled the sexual assault. He explained to the *Tribune* that the song "demonstrates an attitude toward women as basically less than human."[17]

Consider these sample lyrics:

> Yeah, call me the gangster of love. I like bitches,
>   all kinda bitches
> to take off my shirt and pull down my britches.
> If she's got big t _ _ _ _ _ s [slang for breasts] I'll
>   squeeze 'em
> while she sucks my b _ _ _ s [slang for the male
>   genitals] and licks my scrotum.
> If she's got a friend, I'll f _ _ k her, too
> Together we can play a game of switcheroo.

With lyrical content that continually glorifies sexual aggressive behavior, is it any wonder that these boys lived out the sexual fantasy articulated by the Geto Boys? Further, when the American youth culture is saturated with these messages, we shouldn't be surprised at the poll conducted by the Rhode Island Rape Crisis Center which found that the majority of sixth through ninth grade boys felt they had a right to rape a woman, especially when they spent a lot of money on her. (A lot of money was defined as twenty dollars.)

Again, the question of influence brings us to the sad story of John McCollum. Pictured here in his Van Halen T-shirt, John was especially fond

Figure 4.7: John McCollum, suicide victim.

of the music of Ozzy Osbourne (see figure 4.7). In the latter part of 1984, this nineteen-year-old was found shot to death at home on his bed—a victim of suicide. When his parents found him (see figure 4.8) they noted his headphones were still on and plugged into his stereo. Topping the turntable was Ozzy's album with the

Figure 4.8: John was listening to the advice of Ozzy Osbourne at the time of his death.

song "Suicide Solution." Although Ozzy claims the song doesn't advocate suicide, you might want to decide for yourself (see figure 4.9):

> Breaking laws, knocking doors
>   but there's no one at home
> Made your bed, rest your head,
>   but you lie there and moan
> Where to hide, Suicide is the only way out
> Don't you know what it's really about?

Finally, Karen from Minnesota shared her heart with me in a letter:

> I, too, have witnessed the far-reaching effects and influence of today's music on my children. Last year my eighteen-year-old son went to his

daddy's grave and shot himself—his daddy ten years earlier had jumped into the Mississippi River from a bridge ending his life. Both father and son had spent *hours* listening to lyrics from the kind of music you described. As my son's casket was lowered into the ground, his brothers (ages seventeen and twenty) threw into the ground his favorite cassette of Guns N' Roses. I am not saying that disgusting music pulls the trigger of the gun of a suicide—I am saying that it sets the stage and dyes the mind-set of the person. Because the heart is "deceitful above all things and desperately wicked," Satan can use it to gain a victory for his purposes.

Did you catch her key phrase? Depraved music sets the stage. It forms the backdrop. It paves the way for juvenile delinquency—or worse, death.

Am I submitting that John McCollum is dead simply because he listened to an album with a song advocating suicide? Am I suggesting that there is a one-to-one correlation between listening to sexually graphic rap songs and the gang raping of two innocent high school coeds? Am I proposing that Karen's husband and son are dead because of their fondness for fatalistic music? No, not necessarily. However, there is no doubt that these musical products *validated* in the minds of the listeners that, indeed, suicide was an alternative. Thus, a child who is already close to the edge, for whatever reasons, is empowered to take the final step as he listens to an important figure in his life encouraging such a move.

Figure 4.9: Ozzy Osbourne denies he has ever advocated suicide. He is pictured here in Creem, *a teen fan magazine.*

Likewise, when a child hears hours of sexually charged lyrical content—ranging from the rude to the outright raunchy—his or her natural curiosity about the sexual experience is sparked, stoked, and fueled into a roaring flame. Those who seek out and listen to overtly satanic musicians, such as King Diamond, Danzig, and Venom, may not immediately begin to dabble in the occult. However, lyrics by these artists do, in fact, provide a basic introduction to experimentation in witchcraft. Many teens who have come out of satanism trace their exhilarated preoccupation with the occult to bands with satanic themes.

"When a child hears hours of sexually charged lyrical content—ranging from the rude to the outright raunchy—his or her natural curiosity about the sexual experience is sparked, stoked, and fueled into a roaring flame."

Based upon observations of working with troubled teens, Dr. Paul King, a child psychiatrist at the Charter Lakeside Clinic in Memphis, Tennessee, concurs that music can influence young fans. He sees the role of music as shaping their ideas of right and wrong as "the lyrics become their philosophy."[18]

A COMMON SENSE APPROACH

When it comes to the question of music's influence upon the listener, a bit of common sense is in order. We must avoid making two equally disastrous mistakes: (1) blaming *all* of a child's problems upon the impact of his music, and (2) dismissing *any* possible relationship between what a child listens to and what a child does. I might add that not all music affects each of us in the same way. An individual can be profoundly impacted by a song that others find marginally interesting. That's because we're individuals. The fact that some of us are able to emerge relatively unscathed by the scalding venom of a sordid song doesn't mean that others will fair as well. Thus, the question of impact persists.

As we learned in chapter 2, advertisers spend close to half a million dollars on one commercial because they believe they *can* influence the spending habits of those who may tune in to their ad. If advertisers can sell cars, jeans, hamburgers, and appliances in thirty-second spots, what might musicians be selling a child who listens to his "advice" for hours upon hours at a time? Speaking of advertising, consider one more perspective on this question of influence. Sales executives at MTV tell potential advertisers that advertising on MTV will get them results. Yet, proponents of the "anything goes" school of music argue that the videos on MTV with degrading imagery don't have an adverse impact upon the viewer. Would someone please explain how videos with degrading themes have no impact, but the adjacent advertisements (which are, in many cases, designed to look like a typical MTV video) will motivate the viewer to buy a specific product?

Those readers who are still unsure whether music can influence our behavior might find a course in the use of music therapy to teach language most engaging. Did you know that there are only forty-four sounds in the English language? The folks at Hooked on Phonics discovered that the secret to learning a new language is using music. That's why, of course, for centuries grade school teachers have been teaching the ABC's accompanied by music. My sister, Becky Wilson, is a kindergarten teacher who routinely uses her guitar to teach children songs that carry with them specific lessons or messages which she hopes to convey. From "Old McDonald Had a Farm" to "Hickory, Dickory, Dock," any serious student of education recognizes that the combined use of music and words will enhance the learning and memorization process.

Each of us is personally responsible for the choices we make in life. Unfortunately, some folks spend a lifetime living with the consequences of poor choices made during the teen years. The sooner a child learns that his or her entertainment choices have consequences, the sooner he/she will be receptive to the idea of seeking out the best advice on which to base those decisions. As disheartened as you may feel at the moment, don't lose heart. In the chapters that follow, I'll provide practical help for your teens and your family in this most important area of their personal development.

PART TWO

HELP
FOR THIS
GENERATION
AT RISK

5

SETTING THE STANDARD

*I*f you've read this far, most likely you feel overwhelmed by the media assault upon your family, and you may be puzzled as to what you can do about it. Although I cannot offer you a "just add water, mix, and microwave" recipe for the challenges facing you, there are concrete steps that you can take to get your family on track. As you reflect upon the following ideas, you'll probably notice that they will require an added investment of your time. Quite frankly, that's where the rubber meets the road.

In chapter 1, I mentioned the parent who, attempting to pin the blame for his child's delinquency on music, stated: "My kid's all screwed up from heavy metal music and exposure to sexual videos at an early age. Don't blame *me* for his problems. I'm never home!" Unfortunately, children do not become critical thinkers by osmosis. They require our guidance, and guidance necessitates our involvement and time.

So, what can a parent do to cushion the bumps produced by the highway of media hype? There are four essential ingredients to our solution:

1. Set a family standard.

2. Spend plenty of time going "nose to nose" with each child. (I'll explain what that means momentarily.)

3. Incorporate creative concepts into your family routine—concepts that will help your teens think critically about all forms of media.

4. Pray.

This chapter tackles the first two aspects of our solution. Chapter 6 will provide a variety of engaging ideas to help you as you help teens sharpen their critical thinking skills. Then we'll look at a few creative approaches to prayer. Let me encourage you to fight the temptation of skipping ahead to the next chapter because the material we'll be covering in the next few pages sets the stage for the creative concepts listed in chapter 6. As we work toward a solution for the media assault on our adolescents, be sure to keep our goal in view: *Learn to discern.* Or, in the words of Proverbs 3:21 (NIV), "My son, preserve sound judgment and discernment, do not let them out of your sight."

SETTING THE STANDARD

During the mid-eighties, the Alcoa Foundation funded a study to help the leadership at Junior Achievement better understand teenagers and the world they're growing up in. The study's conclusion was most insightful:

> Too many choices, too little help . . . the age of values clarification (as distinguished from values advocacy) has left young people in a quandary. It is clearly a time for specific guidance to youth and for stressing specific values. Young people themselves often feel they have (a) too many choices to make; (b) too few structured means for arriving at decisions; and (c) too little help to get there. In a day when, in the views of many, institutions en masse (in education, service to youth and even religion) have stopped "standing for something," Junior Achievement needs to define and state its standards explicitly.[1]

Parents who provide children with a clear standard of right and wrong empower them to make the best personal and moral choices throughout their life. So, how do *you* know if something is wrong or right? Good or evil? Helpful or harmful? What standard do you use to inform your decision making? The response to this line of questioning may be more significant than you might imagine at first consideration.

If you're like me, teens have argued with you that just because you don't like the music of Madonna, 2 Live Crew, or Prince and because slasher films aren't your cup of tea doesn't make them wrong for those who "appreciate" these forms of media. Furthermore, they dismiss our concern over inappropriate entertainment, stating if you don't like it, just don't listen to it—the age-old "live and let live" approach to life. The use of a standard elevates our evaluation of pop culture above matters of taste. What makes entertainment right and wrong, good or evil, helpful or harmful—indeed, the quest for the source of absolute truth—is where we must begin if we are to groom our children into critical thinkers.

"I cannot offer you a 'just add water, mix, and microwave' recipe for the challenges facing you, there are concrete steps that you can take to get your family on track."

Not long ago, I took part in a state-wide church youth convention in Maine. During my presentation, I asked the one thousand attendees to explain how they know whether something is right or wrong. No kidding, it must have been four or five minutes of head scratching before someone spoke up! I knew we were in trouble when the first youngster suggested rather tentatively, "Ask your dad." "Okay," I responded, "let's consider the problems that that standard would present. What if your dad were Adolf Hitler? Or, by contrast, what if your dad were Billy Graham? You'd get two very different opinions of what was right and wrong behavior." You could feel the audience wrestling with this issue of standards. (Keep in mind, this was a *church* youth convention.) For a moment, I thought someone forgot to coach them in the basics of their faith.

Finally, one youngster spoke up and inquired, "Oh, how about the Bible?" At last! Someone hit the nail on the head. In the discussion that followed, I wanted them to understand how important their standard, the Bible, was and that any old standard wouldn't do. To make this point, I held up and read from a copy of the "personals" section of a newspaper. The first item said, "Attention, couples! Interested in a threesome?" Another stated, "Looking for gay women. Willing to watch or participate. Experiment!" Adultery was the focus of the next personal: "Business men (2) seek married ladies to share occasional afternoons. Discretion assured."

A total of five columns soliciting this sordid behavior from the readership was followed by a disclaimer from the newspaper's editor: "We reserve the right to refuse or edit any personal ad that does not meet the standards of this publication." The kids immediately wondered whether this newspaper had any standards. Actually, yes. Although they listed everything from group sex to voyeurism, apparently they refused to accept ads for sex with children; that's the only form of behavior they considered out of bounds. The point was clear: not all standards are created equal.

CHARACTERISTICS OF
A CRITICAL THINKER

Thus, the first step toward becoming a critical thinker as a Christian is to establish a reliable standard by which all entertainment is evaluated. I am fortunate that my parents elected to use the Bible as our family standard. They, like President Abraham Lincoln, understood the importance of Scripture. Lincoln observed, "All the good from the Savior of the world is communicated through this Book; but for the Book we could not know right from wrong. All the things desirable to man are contained in it."[2]

Over the years, as I've studied the standard of God's Word, I've discovered ten attributes of a critical thinker which you might find beneficial. In the event you did not have parents who worked to nurture these qualities in your formative years, don't despair. A new legacy can be created within your family tree by taking steps to cultivate a discerning spirit in the hearts of your clan.

A critical thinker:

1. Has a firmly developed sense of right and wrong and prefers wisdom over foolish thinking.

2. Understands all music, media, and entertainment is *not* harmless fun.

3. Recognizes that those who are responsible for the creation and promotion of pop entertainment have, in most cases, values which are out of sync with the Judeo-Christian heritage of this country.

4. Doesn't laugh at or enjoy it when his values are attacked, mocked, or undermined by popular culture.

5. Has a habit of asking probing questions about the media he consumes. Doesn't accept the media and entertainment culture as inherently trustworthy.

6. Desires to honor and please the Lord with the choices he makes.

7. Knows that God places a premium on proper communication.

8. Is willing to suffer the loss of a specific entertainment option rather than allow hostile ideas to dominate his mind.

9. Places a premium on his time.

10. When confronted with unfamiliar territory, he proceeds with caution.

Why should a Christian who is determined to be a critical thinker strive to exhibit these ten characteristics? According to God's Word, it's in his best interest to do such.

A critical thinker has a firmly developed sense of right and wrong and prefers wisdom over foolish thinking. In his book *All God's Children and Blue Suede Shoes,* author Kenneth Myers sees the present cultural onslaught as potentially more insidious to the Christian's welfare than outright persecution. He explains, "Enemies that come loudly and visibly are usually much easier to fight than those that are undetectable. Physical affliction (even to the point of death) for the sake of Christ is a heavy cross, but at least it can be readily recognized at the time as a trial of faith. But the erosion of character, the spoiling of innocent pleasures, and the cheapening of life itself that often accompany modern popular culture can occur so subtly that we believe nothing has happened."[3] A critical thinker understands that Hollywood's attack upon his mind is a slow, insidious process—a clear sense of right and wrong keeps him from wallowing in a limbo of gray confusion.

Although not a victim of media inculcation, King David knew the best defense was a good offense. He aggressively studied the Word of the Lord so that he would be wiser than his enemies. In Psalm 119:97–98, 101, 104–105, we see his affection for God's instruction:

O how I love Thy law! It is my mediation all the day. Thy commandments make me wiser than my enemies, for they are ever mine. . . . I have restrained my feet from every evil way, that I may keep Thy word.

> . . . From Thy precepts I get understanding; therefore I hate every false way. Thy word is a lamp to my feet, and a light to my path.

The more familiar we are with God's Word, the better prepared we will be to discern dangerous messages in pop culture.

A critical thinker understands all music, media, and entertainment is not harmless fun. Of the thousands of letters that I've received from teenagers over the last ten years, I'd have to say that a significant portion of those writing have a far too casual opinion of the destructive potential of popular entertainment. Many asserted that if a product or program is labeled "entertainment," it can't hurt you. It's basically harmless. By contrast, the critical thinker isn't so casual about the influence of media upon his life. Why? Because he knows there is a spiritual dimension to all that we experience in this world. According to his standard, a major battle for his heart, his mind, and his soul is being fought in the spiritual realm every day. Ephesians 6:10–13 describes that battle:

> Finally, be strong in the Lord, and in the strength of His might. Put on the full armor of God, that you may be able to stand firm against the schemes of the devil. For our struggle is not against flesh and blood, but against the rulers, against the powers, against the world-forces of this darkness, against the spiritual forces of wickedness in the heavenly places. Therefore, take up the full armor of God, that you may be able to resist in the evil day, and having done everything, to stand firm.

You've probably heard the expression, "Someone loves you and has a wonderful plan for your life." This passage from 1 Peter 5:8, "Be of sober spirit, be on the alert. Your adversary, the devil, prowls about like a roaring lion, seeking someone to devour," provides the flip side of that observation: that the evil one hates us and has a terrible plan for our life. Satan can, and is, using popular music, media, and television to popularize his agenda. A critical thinker recognizes that programming laced with ungodly attitudes has the power to sow the seeds of curiosity about conduct that God knows will harm us. These ideas can open the door to unrighteous thought patterns and, ultimately, destructive behavior.

I might add one related thought. Madonna is *not* the enemy. 2 Live Crew is not the enemy. Calvin Klein is not the enemy. Freddy Krueger and other slasher "stars" are not the enemy, as much as they may resemble him! Ultimately speaking, these popular musicians, movie stars, and

> *"A critical thinker recognizes that*
> *programming laced with ungodly attitudes*
> *has the power to sow the seeds of curiosity*
> *about conduct that God knows will*
> *harm us. These ideas can open the door*
> *to unrighteous thought patterns and,*
> *ultimately, destructive behavior."*

media-makers are mere pawns in Satan's army—for he is our adversary. These folks are victims of his deception.

A critical thinker recognizes that those who are responsible for the creation and promotion of pop entertainment have, in most cases, values which are out of sync with the Judeo-Christian heritage of this country. It's a well-kept secret that only a handful of writers, producers, directors, and business executives control the majority of all programming seen on television. When it comes to personal morality, what do these powerful people believe? How close do their beliefs mirror the mainstream of society?

With the rapid decline in broadcasting standards during the decade of the seventies, professors S. Robert Lichter and Stanley Rothman set out to discover answers to these very questions. Their findings were startling. During 1979 and 1980, they interviewed 240 broadcasters and journalists from national media outlets such as the *New York Times,* the *Wall Street Journal, Time* magazine, *Newsweek,* CBS, NBC, ABC, and PBS (see figure 5.1). Here's some of what they uncovered: "Very few are regular churchgoers. Only 8 percent go to church or synagogue weekly, and 85 percent seldom or never attend religious services. . . . 90 percent agree that a woman has the right to decide for herself whether to have an abortion; 79 percent agree strongly with this pro-choice position."[4]

Although most Americans believe homosexuality is wrong, the Lichter and Rothman team found three-quarters of the media elite believe homosexual behavior is okay. In fact, a mere 9 percent felt strongly that homosexuality is wrong. They also learned that the majority—54 percent—do not regard adultery as wrong, with only 15 percent

Figure 5.1

strongly agreeing that extramarital affairs are immoral. Their conclusion? "Members of the media elite emerge as strong supporters of sexual
freedom or permissiveness."[5]

Without a doubt, the critical thinker embraces a standard that is at
odds with many of those who are responsible for prime-time television
and the entertainment industry. For example, in Galatians 5:16, 19–21
we learn the boundaries of proper conduct:

> But I say, walk by the Spirit, and you will not carry out the desire of
> the flesh. . . . Now the deeds of the flesh are evident, which are:
> immorality, impurity, sensuality, idolatry, sorcery, enmities, strife, jeal-
> ousy, outbursts of anger, disputes, dissensions, factions, envying,
> drunkenness, carousing, and things like these, of which I forewarn you
> just as I have forewarned you that those who practice such things shall
> not inherit the kingdom of God.

Should it really be a surprise that the basic plot of many prime-time
television shows celebrates one or more of the offensive behaviors listed

in Galatians when those who create the programs aren't personally offended by them? Is it really any wonder that the perspective of news reporters tends to be favorable to homosexual radicals and abortionists?

A critical thinker doesn't laugh at or enjoy it when his values are attacked, mocked, or undermined by popular culture. I never cease to be amazed at the number of students who come from "good homes" and even attend private Christian schools who have watched one or more episodes of a teen soft-porn movie—typically, 60 percent of those whom I've surveyed. Hollywood producers have a somewhat rude nickname for these films, films such as *Porky's, Fast Times at Ridgemont High, Revenge of the Nerds,* and *The Last American Virgin.* They refer to these perennial teen favorites as "horny boy" movies—so named for the bountiful supply of images designed to make the hormones of young adolescents pulsate. Not surprisingly, female nudity, voyeurism, and sexual exploration are the three fundamental ingredients for these exercises in carnality. And horny boy films rely upon "plots" that maximize opportunities for displays of unrestrained lust. For example, one of the primary goals of the *Porky's* film series was for Peewee (so named for his small penis) to lose his virginity.

A critical thinker doesn't find these displays of unbridled passion entertaining. Colossians 3:1–2, 5–6 provides the reason why:

> If then you have been raised up with Christ, keep seeking the things above, where Christ is, seated at the right hand of God. Set your mind on the things above, not on the things that are on earth. . . . Therefore, consider the members of your earthly body as dead to immorality, impurity, passion, evil desire, and greed, which amounts to idolatry. For it is on account of these things that the wrath of God will come.

It is inconsistent for a critical thinker to laugh at and enjoy the very thing which prompts God's anger. The more we become Christ-like, the more we will perceive these expressions as direct attacks upon our values and priorities.

By contrast, Romans 1:32 describes the individual who is less discerning. Rather than being offended by such entertainment, he enjoys and wholeheartedly approves of it: "And, although they know the ordinance of God, that those who practice such things are worthy of death, they not only do the same, but also give hearty approval to those who practice them."

A critical thinker makes a habit of asking probing questions about the media he consumes. He doesn't accept the media and entertainment culture as inherently trustworthy. In a prior chapter we discussed the concept of "the directed eye"—the process by which everything we watch on television is shaped to reflect a picture of reality that the producer would have us accept as truth. We learned this inherent trust in the media—that "what we see is reality"—is easily and regularly exploited. Just as the Lord weighs the actions of men, the critical thinker is careful to "test the spirits": "The heart is more deceitful than all else and is desperately sick; who can understand it? I, the LORD, search the heart, I test the mind" (Jeremiah 17:9–10a).

A critical thinker desires to honor and please the Lord with the choices he makes. While I was speaking at a Christian camp, I remember my good friend Thom Hickling (editor of *Expression,* Pittsburgh's Christian newspaper) offering a rather humorous explanation of why he didn't go to R-rated movies when he was a teen. Essentially, he was afraid that the Lord would return right in the middle of the movie and catch him in the audience! Although fear can be a powerful motivator, a critical thinker is also motivated out of a spirit of *gratitude* for the price of redemption which the Lord paid on his behalf. First Peter 1:17b-19 explains it this way:

> Conduct yourselves in fear during the time of your stay upon earth; knowing that you were not redeemed with perishable things like silver or gold from your futile way of life inherited from your forefathers, but with precious blood, as of a lamb unblemished and spotless, the blood of Christ.

Not only is the critical thinker filled with gratitude for the Lord's ultimate act of love, he understands that, according to 1 Corinthians 6:19–20, the living God dwells within him: "Or do you not know that your body is a temple of the Holy Spirit who is in you, whom you have from God, and that you are not your own? For you have been bought with a price: therefore glorify God in your body." Since the Creator of the universe dwells within us, it should be our desire to please Him with the choices we make. And, according to Proverbs 4:23, 26, the Lord will prosper those who walk in the ways of the Lord: "Watch over your heart with all diligence, for from it flow the springs of life. . . . Watch the path of your feet, and all your ways will be established."

A critical thinker knows that God places a premium on proper communication. I've found that teenagers can be quite creative in their attempts to justify deviant lyrics. You've probably heard this argument: "Okay, so the words aren't the greatest. But the musician probably doesn't *really* mean what he's saying anyway." Another line of reasoning used to discount antisocial lyrical imagery has been popularized by various members of the recording industry. While I was debating explicit lyrics before a Maryland state senate subcommittee, musician Frank Zappa argued, "These are only words—words can't hurt anyone."

Rather than make excuses, the critical thinker places a premium on the use of words because he knows that God holds each of us accountable for the things we express—regardless of the impact upon those who hear our speech and whether or not we "mean it." Matthew 12:36–37 cautions us: "And I say to you, that every careless word that men shall speak, they shall render account for it in the day of judgment. For by your words you shall be justified, and by your words you shall be condemned."

A critical thinker is willing to suffer the "loss" of a specific entertainment programming option rather than allow hostile ideas to dominate his mind. It was one of those moments I'll never forget. As I was finishing my talk to a large group of teens at the Creation festival in Mt. Union, Pennsylvania, I spotted a youth wearing a Motley Crüe T-shirt. I had a hunch this guy was a hard-core Crüe fan—a hunch that proved to be correct moments later. His name was Shawn. After inviting him to the front of the audience, I handed Shawn a copy of my Motley Crüe album (a copy I was using for purposes of discussion). With all eyes glued on us, I asked him to break the record in half for me. (Keep in mind this was *my* copy—not his.) He couldn't do it!

I don't mean he wasn't *capable* of breaking it; I mean he couldn't bring himself to destroy a Motley Crüe album, even if it was my copy. Many of us are like Shawn. We know certain movies, albums, or programs aren't good for us, yet for various reasons we have a difficult time casting them aside. One sign of a critical thinker is a willingness to forego offensive entertainment options, much like the example that King David set in Psalm 101:2b–4:

> I will walk within my house in the integrity of my heart. I will set no
> worthless thing before my eyes; I hate the work of those who fall

away; it shall not fasten its grip on me. A perverse heart shall depart from me; I will know no evil.

King David knew that what played in the theater of his mind would shape the habits of his heart. A discerning person works to protect what's playing in his mind.

A critical thinker places a premium on his time. As a young teen, I remember listening to a camp speaker who challenged us to be more actively involved in evangelism. What really struck me was his statement: "Every day of our life, people all across the world are dying. Many who die will spend eternity in hell. Have you done your part to keep others from making that mistake?" His text was taken from Revelation 20:15: "And if anyone's name was not found written in the book of life, he was thrown into the lake of fire." Sitting cross-legged on the floor, I recall thinking, *How can I allow myself to be so selfish as to indulge in endless hours of viewing TV while those around me slip into eternal darkness?*

Thus, a critical thinker, although allowing for periods of recreation, seeks to maximize his time. Since the act of watching television can so easily dominate his schedule, the discerning individual trains himself to make the most of his moments on earth. When the TV beckons, in the back of his mind he hears the words of Ephesians 5:15–16: "Therefore be careful how you walk, not as unwise men, but as wise, making the most of your time, because the days are evil."

A critical thinker, when confronted with unfamiliar territory, proceeds with caution. When working with younger children, you don't have to lay out the "big picture" of all the possible hazardous material they may experience down the road in media-land. Instead, anticipate what's likely to be an issue for them at their particular stage in life. For instance, you can explain to a three-year-old that afternoon soap operas are "bad" without a full-scale description of the adulterous behavior these shows contain. True, there will be an age when that discussion will be necessary. But in the meantime, general principles will suffice.

And yet, at the same time, a wise parent will encourage youngsters to ask questions about things that don't seem proper. Whether on the school bus, at school on the playground, or at a friend's home in the neighborhood, virtually all children will sooner or later be exposed to questionable entertainment. If properly trained, a child will know how to react to this unfamiliar situation. One mother told me this story which makes the point. Her daughter and a group of children were at a friend's

---

"We know certain movies, albums, or programs aren't good for us, yet for various reasons we have a difficult time casting them aside."

---

home sitting in the downstairs playroom watching an "approved" videotape. When the tape was finished, they spotted another videotape that was lying next to the television. As it turned out, the tape was a horror movie and belonged to the adults of that home.

Having never experienced something like this, the children stared at the television in utter shock. In fact, they were so intimidated by what they were watching, they sat motionless through the entire program. With proper training, when confronted with a situation like this, a young child would question whether he should be watching something that his parents hadn't selected.

A critical thinker, regardless of age, is trained to proceed with caution when confronted with unfamiliar territory. I was invited to a bachelor party for a friend. Having never been to one, but fully aware of the scuttlebutt surrounding such events, I proceeded carefully. I also left the party rather early. A discerning spirit takes to heart this insight from Proverbs 2:11: "Discretion will guard you, understanding will watch over you." No matter how they may have wanted to justify it, watching porno movies on the eve of one's wedding is uncalled for. Psalm 32:8 assures us of the Lord's help in making the right choices: "I will instruct you and teach you in the way which you should go; I will counsel you with My eye upon you."

Because the Lord has promised to instruct and counsel us at all times, the critical thinker is miles ahead of those who fall headlong into destructive environments. To this day I pray with regularity a very simple prayer that enables me to have a discerning spirit no matter the circumstance: "Lord, help me to love what You love and hate what You

hate." As He answers that prayer, you and I will experience less of an
appetite for inappropriate media and music.

"NOSE TO NOSE"

Once you've established a family standard, the second primary ingredi-
ent to help your family become more discerning is a concept I call going
"nose to nose" with each child. Have you ever noticed what younger
kids do when their father or mother comes home at the end of a day?
It's interesting to watch how they will jump into their parent's lap and
place their face directly into the face of their mom or dad. This, of
course, facilitates their desire for a one-on-one relationship. You see, by
getting in their parent's face—nose to nose, if you will—they maximize
their chances for intimacy. By way of contrast, if Dad has a chance to
sit down in his easy chair with the newspaper, a child may have to light
the house on fire if he wants to get some attention.

Our high-tech, TV-oriented society is responsible, in part, for the reduction of meaningful parent/child communication. Serving as the assistant
to President Ronald Reagan for Domestic Policy, Gary Bauer observed, "It
may seem incredible, but research tells us that, on an average, mothers
spend four to seven minutes a day educating their children; fathers, zero to
one minute. What are we saying to our children if we allow them to spend
more time watching television by the time they are six than they will spend
talking with their fathers the rest of their lives?"[6]

Take a moment for some personal inventory.

How's the communication with your kids? Are they as much of a
priority as your hobbies, sports, golfing, or other elective activity? Does
the morning conversation around the breakfast table in your home resemble this: "Pass the cornflakes" and "Be home by 10 o'clock"? If so,
it's likely you will need to re-earn the right to be heard. Why work at
better communication with them? When the channels of communication
are strong, dialogue about difficult subjects is easier to handle.

So, what can be done to rebuild the bridge of good communication?
Here are a few tips to get you started:

   1. As often as possible, engage your children in discussions on a
      variety of subjects. Talk about anything: world events, local

news, happenings at school or church. When it comes time to address popular music, movies, or television, you'll have demonstrated that you care about all aspects of their lives, not just "their" music.

2. Make a date with your son or daughter for breakfast before school. Use the time to really listen, not preach. When I was a child, since there were five of us DeMoss kids, my dad and mom made an effort to take each of us out for a special meal. Boy, did that time seem to go by quickly!

3. Surprise them by showing up on their turf. Many parents will try at least once in a while to go to a soccer, basketball, or baseball game during the season, which is a real boost to their children's morale. Likewise, attending a sports practice or drama rehearsal unannounced communicates to them that you think they're important.

4. Talking about issues is fine, but so is incorporating times of play, fun, and laughter. Learn how to enjoy each other. My dad holds several master's degrees and is a graduate of seminary. There's no doubt that he could easily dominate our times together with heady discussion. Instead, he made time to let his hair down and be playful with us. That's why even today I consider him (and my mother) to be my best friends.

5. Hug 'em. I cannot think of a more important device that will build self-confidence, character, and healthy dialogue than a warm hug. I've worked with many kids who never experienced that simple treasure.

6. And, for a real treat, instead of our riding the bus for an hour, my dad would drive us to school from time to time before going to work. Whenever possible, this activity could help you to "connect" to your children's "workplace."

7. If you have to work on weekends at the office, bring one of the kids along. When I was a child, my dad did exactly that with me. He would set me up with a typewriter, paper, and plenty of erase tabs. He also showed me how to use the copier (I had already mastered the use of the hot cocoa machine), so I was

really in business. These semi-regular visits to the office helped me feel more "connected" to him and his work.

The bottom line of going nose to nose is to affirm your children's value as individuals, to demonstrate that you are interested in their ideas, their views, and their issues. As you make the time to be with them one-on-one, you can work to elevate their level of self-esteem and build their confidence. Strengthening the dialogue between you and them will help them feel comfortable discussing a wide range of subjects—including, one day, that all-important area of music and entertainment.

MORE THAN A PHASE

A reporter from Burlington, Ontario, once quizzed me about the negative trends in the Canadian youth entertainment culture. After demonstrating that Canada appears to have embraced much of the American youth culture, I explained how imperative it was for parents to be involved with their teenagers, assisting them to make the best entertainment decisions. Not fully convinced that parental involvement was necessary, she asked, "Don't you think that a teenager's exploration of the 'darker' side of films, music, and entertainment is a phase which all adolescents go through? Isn't it a natural part of their childhood experience—something they'll ultimately grow out of?" I wish it were that simple.

Yes, in some ways, it *is* a phase. But adolescence is a season of life fraught with the consequences and casualties of poor decision making. Youth fatality statistics demonstrate that, unfortunately, contrary to this reporter's assumption, all teens don't make it *through* these turbulent years. Many embrace the destructive philosophies popularized by the world of entertainment and ultimately self-destruct—victims of suicide, accident, or crime. Others, who may be more fortunate and manage to make it through, fall into patterns of addiction with lifelong consequences. Few leave their adolescent years unscathed.

Once you've established a family standard, and after you've rebuilt the channels of good communication with the kids, you're in the best position to incorporate creative ideas that can fine-tune their discernment skills and prepare them for a lifetime of Christian service.

6 *GETTING A GRIP*

*D*_{ear Bob,}

I'm a fourteen-year-old girl who used to be a preppy little "Christian" last year. I fell in love with a Christian guy—who is now nineteen and happened to be my youth minister for that summer of 1990. He did everything to help me with my walk with God. I used to be beaten (and sometimes still am) by my mother, and he often—if not always, comforted me. He tried to get me to tell the authorities about my family problems and my abuse, but I refused.

My parents became Christians and then became church leaders. What I couldn't understand was how they can be leaders of God's house and still beat me and ridicule me at home. That's when I began to drift away from God completely. So here I am, now a year later, and I believe that there isn't such a thing as a God or Jesus or a Holy Ghost. It's all a fool's imagination—just something to believe in.

The further I drift away, none of the Christians that I knew seem to want to help bring me back—they just don't care. Instead, they look down at me just because I listen to heavy metal and sixties rock 'n' roll such as the Doors (my fav band), and because I've drunk, smoked, and done a little drugs. I do it all basically out of rebellion and out of self-destruction.

I've tried to commit suicide before, but I couldn't go through with it. I'm kind of obsessed with my death because it means that I'll be able to get out of this life. I'll be able to leave my life forever. But whenever I try to think realistically, I know that I won't go to Heaven. And when I look at myself closely in the mirror, all I can say is, "Goddamn, you're only fourteen!" But, like I say, no one cares. Isn't it a Christian's responsibility to bring people to the Lord and not away from Him? How do I know there's a Jesus when I can't even see Him through the hearts of "Christian" parents? Please help me.

ta   ta   ta

I've included fourteen-year-old Dorothy's letter for several reasons. If you skipped—or breezed over—the last chapter, you might have missed the first two steps necessary if you want to get a grip on this runaway culture and its devastating impact on our kids: set a family standard and build stronger communication bridges with each child. Another motive for reprinting her letter is to remind us that our children are not little "projects" that need work, even if they resemble them! They're precious people who need to know that we believe in them, love them, and desire the best for their lives.

I've spent the better part of ten years working to equip parents, educators, and civic leaders with the tools to deter the lifelong consequences of delinquency among our youth. I've been invited as a guest speaker to address and participate in the White House Conference for a Drug-Free America, President Reagan's Child Safety Partnership, and the Office of Juvenile Justice and Delinquency Prevention branch of the U.S. Justice Department. I've studied plenty of programs aimed at reducing the rate of childhood disorders. I still believe that many of the self-destructive behaviors children like Dorothy engage in would be minimized—if not eliminated all together—if the significant adult(s) in their life was more involved in building their self-esteem and demonstrating Christ's love to them.

I don't want us to be naive on this point. There is a degree of personal choice and accountability here. On one hand, parents should not feel like failures if, after they've worked hard to teach their children to be discerning Christians, the child decides to abandon his upbringing. On the other hand, it *is* our duty to provide them with a godly role model and the proper training so that they have the best information necessary to make the right choices.

As you engage your children with the creative ideas listed in this chapter, there are three ground rules I'd like to propose:

1. Whenever possible, use a tangible example—a visual aid—for discussion purposes.

2. Don't spoon-feed the correct answers to your children. Allow them to wrestle with the ideas. Assume the role of "coach" in your discussions. Let *them* play the game.

3. Keep in mind, no idea is a "dumb" idea. Encourage children to express even wrong answers. Avoid ridicule when a youngster "doesn't get it" immediately.

Having said that, consider these creative ideas that can assist you in this task of teaching discernment. I've grouped these suggestions to cor-

---

"Parents should not feel like failures if, after they've worked hard to teach their children to be discerning Christians, the child decides to abandon his upbringing."

---

relate with the three voices of the culture: advertising, television and films, and music.

ADVERTISING: TO TELL THE TRUTH

In chapter 2 we examined two types of advertisements: those that undermine the self-esteem of our daughters and ads that promote a warped perspective of human sexual conduct. There are many other considerations about the world of advertising that you can readily discuss with children. Here are a few creative ideas to get you started.

Don't Buy One of the Five Big Lies

From time to time, my dad would bring a print ad to the dinner table for our study. His purpose was to help us discover which of the "five big lies" it contained. Learning to identify the underlying philosophy of an advertisement helps us cut through the haze to the heart of what's really being sold.

Lie 1: Materialism. The most important thing in life is the ownership of possessions. Through the accumulation of material things we can, in effect, buy happiness. ("Now that you've arrived—drive Cadillac." Note: This ad *doesn't* say "*a* Cadillac.")

Lie 2: Existentialism. Live for the moment; it's all that you have. ("You only go around once in life so grab for all the gusto!")

Lie 3: Individualism. The most important person in life is you—wonderful you! You deserve your fair share. ("You *deserve* a break today. . . .")

Lie 4: Hedonism. Pleasure, happiness, and fun are the primary purposes of life. Pursue pleasure; minimize discomfort. ("Go ahead—spoil yourself in satin.")

Lie 5: Secularism. This view of life ignores all religious considerations. God is not significant. (You'll notice these types of ads especially around the traditionally religious holidays of Thanksgiving, Christmas, and Easter.)

Count the Changes

One evening, as your family sits down to view television, make a group project of counting the number of times that the picture changes during a thirty-second commercial message. A typical hour of prime-time television viewing includes eighteen minutes of commercials, so you'll have plenty of opportunities to work up an average. If you're watching MTV, many commercials move so quickly it might be impossible to count them all!

Afterward, ask the family a series of questions, such as: Why does the advertiser change the picture about once every three seconds? Further, how much time does that give to carefully evaluate the subtle messages implied in each clip? If you own a videotape player you might consider recording a series of commercials. Then, as you play them back, you have the ability to freeze each frame to more carefully examine and discuss what feelings the advertiser is attempting to provoke or manipulate in us as consumers.

Interact with the Ads

Whether in print, radio, or television, teach children to pay close attention to the promises contained in many ads. Have them consider: Is the ad implying that you'll be happier, better liked, or closer to the "in crowd" if you buy this product? Is the advertiser attempting to exploit your feelings? Is he trying to make you dissatisfied with what you now have so that you'll spend money on his product? Is shouting at the TV

"Whether in print, radio, or television, teach children to pay close attention to the promises contained in many ads."

---

during a commercial—"Forget it pal, I'm happy with what I have"— such a bad idea?

Cut Through the Gimmicks

Like the five big lies, there are three advertising techniques or gimmicks that are often used which have nothing to do with the inherent value of a product. Bring a variety of magazines to the table and give one to each family member. Set a time limit and have everyone search for these gimmicks.

Gimmick 1: Get on the bandwagon. "Everyone's doing it." The implication is "and so should you," or "and that makes it right." Sun Country wine coolers once urged viewers to "Join the party!"—complete with pictures of dozens of bathing beauties on the beach. Well, now, who wants to be left out of a party? Their goal is to get us to think, *Look's like everyone's having such a great time . . . better get on the bandwagon and have some fun.* A discerning person doesn't make decisions to purchase or do something simply because many others are.

Gimmick 2: Image projection. Actually, you really aren't buying a product in this case. Rather, the advertiser is projecting an image or idea that the consumer likes to be associated with. The way this works is simple. The ad implies "buy our product and you'll be just like the image we've constructed." Cigarette advertisers tend to rely heavily on this gimmick (see figure 6.1). After all, what is a cigarette? It's nothing more than a dried-up weed that produces cancer, lung disorders, and gum disease. Not exactly an easy product to sell given its deadly reputation, so tobacco companies use macho men and cosmopolitan women to sell their smokes.

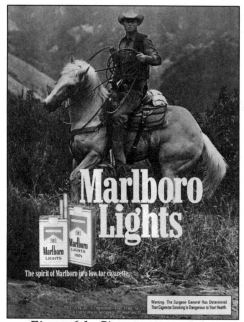

Figure 6.1: Cigarette companies sell a lifestyle, not a product.

When my parents pointed this gimmick out to us, I was fascinated to see how right they were. Virtually all tobacco ads use a tiny portion of their ad space for the actual box of cigarettes, especially compared to the image that's projected around it. A discerning individual can see through this smoke screen.

Gimmick 3: Testimonial. A famous person places his or her "stamp of approval" on a given product. The implication is that "since Joe Star uses 'brand x' you should, too." Our television screens are saturated with testimonials: comedian Bill Cosby eating Jello pudding, basketball star Michael Jordon shooting hoops in his Air Nikes, baseball coach Tommy Lasorda drinking his Ultra Slim Fast, and musician Michael Jackson endorsing Pepsi—perhaps the most memorable abuse of a testimonial. He doesn't even drink Pepsi because of the high sugar content!

A discerning person makes purchasing decisions based on the merits and quality of a product, not because an overpaid spokesman advocates it.

Does the Girl Come with the Car?

Advertisers know how to package their products with lots of "sex appeal." That's why car ads place beautiful blondes on the hood, pants companies find voluptuous "babes" to wear their skin-tight jeans, and perfume manufacturers parade women with sultry eyes across the TV screen to entice us. As kids, when confronted by these types of ads, we used to respond: "Let me guess. Batteries and the girl aren't included with the car." The use of humor can defuse this obvious manipulation tactic.

MOVIES AND TELEVISION:
HOW TO MANAGE THE
SILVER SCREEN

Here's a humorous, but painfully true, story that my editor shared from personal experience. He, too, was concerned about the growing impact of TV upon his marriage and his four daughters. One night, after the children went to bed, he took decisive action to rid the home of this menace. I'm sure his wife must have looked puzzled. One moment they were sitting quietly together in their family room. The next minute, Mike picked up the TV, turned it sideways (facedown), and dropped it on the floor.

But it didn't break. "Man, it's amazing how durable this thing is," he said. Mike rushed out of the room, went downstairs to get a hammer (by now, his wife thought he was completely off his rocker!) which he then threw into the TV screen. This time he was effective. In the morning his daughters saw their now unusable TV set on the family room floor. As Mike tells it, they stood around in silence and actually cried over the loss of their friend! Several weeks later, they all looked back and laughed.

Now, don't panic. When it comes to getting unplugged from the television, I'm not suggesting that every family should go to such drastic measures. Indeed, for some families, going cold turkey is the best and only way to get a handle on the box. However, let me propose twelve ideas that may accomplish the same goal, with less glass to clean up!

As you consider these creative ideas to curb the tube, don't feel like you must implement all of them or none at all. You'll be amazed at the difference in your family life when you execute even one of the suggestions.

Establish a TV-Usage Policy

When we were younger, my parents limited our viewing to one hour per day. (And, for the most part, we were not permitted to watch television on Sundays.) What's more, our shows had to be approved in advance. You can do the same with your children using a local program guide. There are several benefits to this system. First, children are taught to budget their time. You may recall in the last chapter we learned that a discerning person places a premium on his time. Forming good habits while children are young is the best place to begin.

You might get a kick out of this. As a child, I was not permitted to watch "Gilligan's Island." Why? Back then, Ginger was a bit too sexy for our family standard. Amazingly, I survived, and your kids will, too, when you cross off offensive shows from their list. Another benefit to having programs preapproved is that it prevents hours of "vegging" in front of the tube—a practice that produces grumpy, unproductive children.

By the way, be sure to have others enforce your rules, including the baby-sitter. Don't assume that a baby-sitter will know and respect your family's television policy if you don't explain what it is. One mother told me how her six-year-old son was suffering from a series of nightmares. Looking closer, they discovered that the twelve-year-old Christian baby-sitter had viewed a horror movie with the little boy alongside her on the sofa. Apparently, she did not come from a home that taught the principles of discernment. Be sure to establish a TV standard even for those who care for your youngsters (day-care centers included!).

Don't Place a TV in the Children's Bedroom

In the early days of television, if a family could afford to own one, they placed it in a public place where all could see what was playing. Today, with the advent of small portable TVs and Sony "Watchman"-type products, some parents wrongly believe they're doing the family a favor by wiring the kids' room with cable. In effect, what we're doing is allowing our children to be in a private world of their own, one that excludes our involvement.

On many occasions, I've been the guest at a friend's home where the parents allowed their children to huddle together around a TV set for hours at a time with no supervision. This practice violates all the principles of teaching sound discernment. If you have numerous TVs around the house, consider selling all but one of them, which you locate in a public place (and use the money saved to reduce credit card debt).

Don't Place a TV in Your Bedroom

Okay, so I won't score many points with that suggestion. However, there are a number of good reasons to consider this. First, you will set a good example for the children. Second, I've been told by numerous couples that a television in the bedroom can interrupt time for much-needed dialogue. For most adults, the bedroom at night provides the only time of day when parents are not surrounded by children. A TV in your master bedroom is guaranteed to stifle your privacy.

Post Psalm 101:3 Above the Set

In a previous chapter, I shared the important perspective from King David found in this verse: "I will set no worthless thing before my eyes;

"Another benefit to having programs preapproved is that it prevents hours of 'vegging' in front of the tube—a practice that produces grumpy, unproductive children."

I hate the work of those who fall away; it shall not fasten its grip on me." Posting this verse in big type above the television set in your home serves as a friendly reminder from our Sponsor about the kinds of things a discerning person ought to avoid viewing.

Never Use the TV as a Baby-sitter

When you're too tired to interact with the children, don't sit them in front of the TV for a few hours. Of course, it's easy for me to suggest this because as I write, I have no children. However, I have been told by those who do, it is far better to have a number of activities on standby to engage the kids (drawing, reading, stories on cassette tape for nap-time listening) rather than permitting them to watch several hours of pointless cartoons.

Purge Your Cable Package

Depending on how radical you're feeling, consider cancelling your HBO, Showtime, or Cinemax cable service. If you really miss these channels (by the way, they all air unedited R-rated fare—and worse), you can always reorder them. My guess is your family will be all the better for it if you suspend these services. While you're on a roll, either block or dump MTV.

Hunt for Christian Heroes

Question: When was the last time you saw a Christian portrayed in a positive, even desirable light on TV? Hint: Rare to never. That's why Focus on the Family's film division has created the exciting live-action and animation video series entitled *McGee and Me*. Other organizations have produced similar videos featuring biblical heroes. By building a home video library with Christian heroes, your children will have their values reinforced by what they watch.

Make a List of Alternative Activities

One reason Americans consume so much television is its ability to entertain us on a moment's notice. When you have some energy, write down a list of alternative activities that your family could do instead of staring into a flickering screen for those times when you don't have the energy to think creatively. Post these ideas next to the television.

Replan Your Floor Plan

Exhibit A (see figure 6.2) features the typical floor plan most Americans use in their family or recreation room. You might be surprised how much we can learn about a person's priorities simply by looking at the arrangement of his or her furniture. In this case, using the furniture as your clue, what's the center of attention in this home? Answer: the television. All of the chairs are placed to maximize extended periods of viewing. Chances are, the chairs are soft, cozy, and comfortable.

To minimize the amount of time spent watching the box—for those who dare, move a chair. In Exhibit B (see figure 6.3), you'll notice the arrangement of furniture is similar to Exhibit A but with one major difference. There's a sofa directly in front of the boob tube—facing away from the set. Now what's the center of attention? Answer: each other. Chances are, when someone visits your home, they will ask, "What's wrong? TV broken?" To which you respond, "Nope. You see, we have a policy in our home that requires the TV to speak and act as a family member. And, until it learns to behave properly, it's being punished in the corner!"

Figure 6.2: Exhibit A

If rearranging the furniture in your home according to Exhibit B is too progressive a concept, consider at least using uncomfortable, hard-back chairs. You'll definitely find people spending less time watching if the seats are stiff. You could also save on the energy bill if you don't heat or cool the room to perfection.

Protect Kids from Porn at the Video Store

If your family is a member of a local video rental store, consider soliciting help from the management. Ask them to restrict the rental of R, X, NC-17 (and maybe even PG-13) to your children. There's also the issue of unrated videotapes, which gets a bit confusing. In the early days of motion pictures, films were not rated. Why? Because virtually all films provided acceptable viewing for the entire family.

Not so today. Many films released by Hollywood in the unrated category contain sexually graphic, violent, or other degrading elements. To forbid the rental of all unrated titles would potentially wipe out all of the classic movies along with the current offenders. And yet, the management should be notified of your desire to keep the offenders out of the hands of your children.

Figure 6.3: Exhibit B

Be Your Own Editor

Technology can be a wonderful thing. Armed with a video player, you can begin to build a video library of family-edited films—films that *you* edit yourself! Here's how it works. Most VCRs have the ability to record audio and video signals. Let's say you've purchased a film which contains several inappropriate uses of the word *damn*, but otherwise it is a good family film. You can erase just the audio track—that's the part of the tape where the audio information is recorded—and replace it with silence. Or, if you're clever, there's a way for you to insert your own word, like *shucks* or *rats*.

For the films that have one inappropriate bedroom scene or brief glimpse of nudity, you can still be your own editor. Time the segment in question and then record over both the audio and video track. As long as the producers in Hollywood insist on ruining perfectly wonderful films with one or two vulgarities or unsuitable segments, you may find this option a lifesaver.

Pattern After Patton

When I was twelve, my dad took me to see the movie *Patton,* featuring George C. Scott. Keep in mind I never heard my parents use "spicy" language in our home—oh, except once. My father stubbed his toe and proceeded to use the "d" word. I promptly ran to my bedroom to pray that he wouldn't go to hell! On the whole, foul language was not something I lived with as a child. So, imagine my surprise as I sat at the theater next to Dad with my popcorn and cold drink in hand as Patton strolled onto the screen swearing a blue streak!

Two thoughts went immediately through my mind. First, I felt embarrassed, particularly for my dad! *Poor Pops. He's hearing words he's never heard before.* My second thought was, *At any minute, Dad is going to make us rush out of the theater and demand our money back from the management*—making a scene sure to mortify me. Actually, my fears were unfounded. Much to my amazement my father *had* heard foul language in his lifetime. And, no, we didn't run for the doors either.

As it turned out, my father took me to this film in order to discuss the appropriate use of language, the themes of war, peace, and other topics I've long since forgotten. What I do remember is the most important lesson of all: Dad was willing to spend time on my turf. I'll never forget that night sitting at the pizza parlor. I was grateful that my dad, as busy as he was, wanted to help me sharpen my critical thinking skills, especially in the area of films.

You can do the same with your children. Of course, be selective in the choice of film. It might be a good idea to preview any movie you plan to use as a teaching aid with children. This ensures that you'll be comfortable with what they will be seeing. It might also give you an opportunity to be mentally prepared for the questions they're likely to ask. It goes without saying that certain films are out of bounds for any reason. A child can be taught that "adult" porno movies are degrading and evil without watching one.

MAKING THE MOST OUT OF MUSIC

As you challenge your teens to be discerning in this, the third voice of the culture, may I encourage you to avoid acting as if you have all the answers. Be honest. Admit that you might not know everything there is to know about every artist. At the same time, let them know that you're there to discover together with them what music is appropriate for your home. Too many parents force their children to walk away mad over their dogmatic, overbearing approach. Our goal is to *engage* them, not propel them into isolation.

Unload the Losers: a Record Buy-Back Policy

If there has been no prior enforcement of a family standard pertaining to the music children were allowed to purchase, resist the temptation to sneak into their bedrooms to smash all of their tapes. Although you might feel better doing so, that violation of their personal space will likely drive a wedge of resentment between you and them, and that's exactly what we need to avoid (see figure 6.4).

Here's an idea to get things back to square one. The goal of this step is to demonstrate fair play. Begin by declaring a period of amnesty. Announce that you—as their loving, kind, wonderful, caring, gracious,

"YOU MEAN YOU COULDN'T HEAR THEIR SUBLIMINAL MESSAGE, 'THROW ME AWAY, THROW ME AWAY'?"

Figure 6.4

and generous parents—are willing to buy back all the records, tapes, and CDs that don't meet your family standard. After all, can we blame them for the choices they've made if we haven't given them the guidance necessary to make the right selections?

Of course, you do this record buy-back procedure at depreciated rates; these *are* used goods! You still may have to mortgage the house, but the children cannot call you inequitable. Once the home is cleaned up, proceed to the next step.

Select Records Responsibly

After you've unloaded the losers in the previous step, announce to the children that they may purchase any record, tape, or CD that they want on one condition: it cannot violate your family standard. If, upon review of the record, you find it to be trash, your children will be out the cash! This, of course, will encourage teens to be more selective at the point of purchase.

For a variety of reasons, you won't be able to accompany your youth every time they go shopping for music. By instilling the principles of responsible record buying in them, you'll be ahead of the game when it comes time to enforce the family standard. I believe you might be able to identify with this letter from a homemaker who makes this point so well:

> I am a housewife, mother of three sons ages ten, eleven, and fourteen. My oldest bought a new tape a couple of weeks ago. Ordinarily I would have been with him, but it was hot, I was tired, so I waited in our mini-van. Later that evening, I asked to see the tape; he knows I have to okay it.
>
> It was by a group with which I was unfamiliar: Digital Underground. First, I read the "objectionable material" warning, then saw the picture inside—the man with two women—then something about "sex side" on one side of the tape. With my son watching (a rather sickly look on his face), I started to play the tape. I couldn't get through the first song. I destroyed the tape; my son knows I'll do that when he brings garbage home.

Do you see the wisdom of this woman? Somewhere along the line she made it clear what the ground rules were. Her son *knew in advance* how she would respond if, and when, he purchased an unacceptable tape. When a child is taught to apply the principles of his faith to the entertainment choices he makes, he receives a gift of discernment that will accompany him for a lifetime. King David was concerned that all of his thoughts and words please his Heavenly Father. In Psalm 19:14 (NIV), David sang, "May the words of my mouth and the meditation of my heart be pleasing in your sight, O LORD, my Rock and my Redeemer." If your children can sing along with King David on that song, chances are they'll be significantly more careful with the other tunes they put on their tongues.

Listen Up . . . and Be a Good Listener

Don't read the paper, watch television, or engage in some other activity while your child shares his or her concerns about music with you. Respect your child's position. I'm not saying you have to agree with him when he wants to discuss current events in music, but influencing his ideas will be easier if mutual respect remains intact. My father and mother took this a step further. Instead of us children always initiating the questions, they'd bring home a popular album for us to discuss as a family.

I can remember sitting around our living room listening to the sound track for the hit musical *Jesus Christ Superstar*. As we listened to this double-record set, my folks asked us a series of questions: "What portion of this account is biblically authentic? Where is it inaccurate? How does it expand or maybe take away from your understanding of Pilate and the different characters surrounding Christ's life on earth? How did they make Jesus look? Was He God incarnate or simply a man on a mission who went crazy toward the end of his life?" This process is one of the most important methods of imparting and inculcating a discerning spirit.

Share the Concert Experience

Let's say a child asks, "Mom, can I go to the New Kids on the Block concert?" How do you handle that one? If you respond, "No, and that's final," you appear unreasonable. After all, these musicians may be recording positive music. I'd like to propose an option instead of simply saying "Okay" or "No way." Have your child write out a four-hundred-word essay explaining why he'd like to see this particular band. Ask him or her to provide you with details about the group: their style of music, names of any albums or songs that he's familiar with, and so on. If, after reading his or her analysis, you believe that the show will be appropriate, have him purchase two tickets—one for him and one for you. Offer to provide the transportation and pizza after the show.

There are a number of benefits in sharing the concert experience. First, it provides important "nose to nose" time. Second, you are in the best position to discuss future concerts if you share a history. ("Remember at the so-and-so concert how the lead singer used a surprising amount of vulgarities? Is that the kind of program we want to support with our money?")

"Don't read the paper, watch television, or engage in some other activity while your child shares his or her concerns about music with you. Respect your child's position."

Third, you'll have the opportunity to talk not only about what's happening on stage but what's happening around the concert hall. In the summer of 1991, three children were crushed to death at an AC/DC concert as the crowd crammed together in front of the stage. One of the youngsters who died was twelve; it was his first and last concert. As I read the news account I couldn't help but wonder: Where was his dad? Why wasn't one of his parents on hand to teach him that it's unsafe to be trapped in a crowd like that?

A fourth benefit comes down the road. There will come a day when they will grow up and no longer be under your direct supervision. They may elect to go to concerts that you might not approve, that may endanger their safety. Sharing the concert experience while they are young can give them discerning eyes for the days when you're not with them.

Encourage Teens to Become "Rock Star Missionaries"

As a child, I asked my dad this question: "If Satan is behind all of the evil in the world, and if he is keeping people from heaven, why don't we just pray that the devil gets saved?" (Nobody has ever accused me of being unambitious.) Since Satan's fate is sealed, a better use of our energies might be to pray for those musicians still caught in his evil grasp.

With this in mind, several years ago I began to challenge teens to become "Rock Star Missionaries." It's so simple and anyone can do it. All it takes is paper, pen, postage, and prayer.

Most albums provide an address where fans can write the band. You might also find fan club address listings in magazines like *Hit Parader, Creem, Star Hits, Rip,* or *Circus.* Have your teen begin by sharing with the musician what it means to be a believer and indicate that he or she will be praying for him. After mailing the letter, put the artist's name on the refrigerator and pray for him or her often. Serious rock star missionaries will write the performer more than once, even as much as once a month.

Jesus said, "There is a saying, 'Love your *friends* and hate your enemies.' But I say: Love your *enemies!* Pray for those who *persecute* you" (Matthew 5:43–44, emphasis added, LB). As much as we may be angered by the work of musicians who don't follow Jesus, we're still charged with the responsibility of praying for them. Wouldn't it be exciting if a popular performer made a commitment to Christ as a result of your child's initiative and persistence? Once in a while a teen has said to me, "Oh, come now, Bob. What are the chances of this really working?" Frankly, that's up to God, but the likelihood is increased when we do our part.

In case you're wondering what becoming a rock star missionary has to do with sharpening discernment, consider this: the process helps Christian teenagers see the philosophical differences between their beliefs and that of the unsaved musician. And second, they become active rather than passive. They begin to look differently at the popular musician. No longer is the artist a "superstar"; he's a person with an eternal destiny that needs guidance. Thus, feelings of compassion are produced in the heart of the teen. Ultimately, the Christian teenager comes to see that he has more on the ball than the mega-star.

Be Cautious, Yet Flexible

This might be a stretch for some readers, but I firmly believe that not *all* music recorded by non-Christians is communicating negative, antisocial, or ungodly ideas. It's both unfair and inaccurate to assume that *every* album recorded by an unbeliever that your child purchases contains indecent material. By contrast, a significant portion of artists today are singing about social concerns, such as the plight of the homeless, injustice, poverty, illiteracy, fidelity, hunger, and a host of other important matters.

Truth is truth, regardless of who expresses it. God's common grace allows even the unregenerate to make correct observations about our world. I remember in high school listening to a song by Billy Joel called "Just the Way You Are." I was struck by the fact that this popular secular musician would promote the notion of a friendship devoid of the pressure to change each other in order to be acceptable. In a world that places a premium on looking, smelling, and dressing to impress, Joel's message was a breath of fresh air and entirely consistent with biblical teaching.

I like how Dana Key (lead singer for the Christian rock band Degarmo and Key) addresses this question of listening to secular music. Dana writes:

> Many people misunderstand the distinction between sacred and secular. We Christians have failed to see that the whole earth is the Lord's—along with everything in it. So we fall into the trap of compartmentalizing the world into sacred and secular. We think: Going to church is spiritual, but going to work is secular. In God's eyes, going to work is just as much a spiritual duty as going to church. . . . God's truth is no different from other truths, such as the truth that 2+2=4. The math statement is not "secular" truth, because all truth—theological or mathematical—is God's.[1]

Key offers some added advice on how to select music recorded by unbelievers: "Listen to music of virtue and positive moral value. Listen to music that is performed with skill. Listen to music that helps you love God more, whether or not it is full of Christian lingo."[2] A child can be taught how to discern the difference between secular music that edifies from that which exploits the human spirit.

Follow the Beat of a Different Drummer

I am a firm advocate of the blessings that listening to contemporary Christian music (CCM) can bring to our spirit. As you work to help teens change their tunes, check out the options that await them at a local Christian bookstore. (As you may know, there are a few who disagree with me on this point. That's why the next chapter is devoted to the concerns some have raised over CCM.)

Instill an Interest in Instruments

I am thankful that my parents encouraged each of us five children to take up an instrument. To this day, whenever our clan gets together, we'll pull out the instruments and "jam," sometimes for hours. I believe that dependency on store-bought recordings is reduced as children participate in the creative process by performing their own music.

Thanks to my parents' support, I went a step farther than just a love of playing guitar. I recorded and pressed my first album in the tenth grade—and sold out! (Of course, we pressed only two copies.) To work through that process—recording in a studio, watching the custom pressing plant convert my tape to vinyl, designing the album jacket—taught me a number of invaluable lessons about the workings of the record business.

Give Them God's Word

As mentioned in the last chapter, give them a standard by which they can make sound judgments; avoid the hit list approach. There are many biblical references that will provide needed guidance. These particular passages will come in handy as you set the standard on premarital sex, witchcraft, and alcohol consumption: Galatians 5:16–21, Colossians 3:1–8, James 3:6–10, and Ephesians 6:10–13. At the same time, remember to teach them that little prayer: "Lord, help me to love what You love and hate what You hate." This invitation for God's direction is sure to cultivate a discerning spirit in all who request His guidance.

CONCLUSION

Now that you've read this far, you might feel like there's quite a lot of work ahead of you. I can understand those feelings. But, let me encourage you to think in terms of proceeding *one step at a time*—take one or two of these ideas and begin to incorporate them into the family routine. Some ideas require less energy, so why not start with them. For example, posting Psalm 101:3 above the television set requires a few minutes! Don't feel like you must adopt every idea immediately. This is a marathon, not a fifty-yard dash.

Have you ever attempted to lose weight? Think of the person who wants to lose forty pounds. Weight loss is a process that requires a change in eating habits and a higher level of commitment to exercise. Likewise, helping your family members to become critical thinkers rather than remain passive consumers of popular entertainment requires a change in habits and priorities, both of which will take time. When-ever I was faced with a big assignment, my mom used to say, "Bob, a job begun is a job half done."

"A child can be taught how to discern the difference between secular music that edifies from that which exploits the human spirit."

Let me encourage you to get out a pen and mark up the ideas we've just studied. Make changes, adaptions, or additions, and refer to the list as often as needed. By no means do I have all of the answers or a corner on the market of helpful ideas. So be creative! But by all means get a *start*. And don't forget to invite the Lord to give you the resolve to go the distance.

DANCING TO THE BEAT OF A DIFFERENT DRUMMER

D*ear Bob,*

I'm a fifteen-year-old teen from a small midwestern town. I really respect what you have to say—most of the time. However, you are undoubtedly ignorant about something important—which is why I'm writing. Recently, you have been promoting "Christian" rock music. What you may not know is that Satan is using this "Christian" rock to get to "Christian" kids (and the church as a whole) through the back door.

It seems innocent, I know. But the spirit behind "Christian" rock has the word phony written all over it. What I hate most about "Christian" rock is that the messages are vague and meaningless. I was literally pulled out of the "Christian" rock mess by the Holy Spirit Himself, who told me personally that this "Christian" rock is evil.

ફ‍ે   ફ‍ે   ફ‍ે

The writer of this note, Bryan, is not alone in his position. He reminds me of some of the parents who have contacted me to debate the validity of contemporary Christian music. One adult explained that God couldn't possibly use *any* contemporary form of music for the advancement of the kingdom, stating, "Christ-honoring music does not come in the world's packages known as rap and metal."

For some readers, the following pages may be the most controversial part of our study together. Quite honestly, it's a portion of the book that I wish I didn't have to spend time writing (although I do so gladly). Why? Because I've watched a small portion of Christendom spread rumors about, even outright hatred for, Christian musicians who have devoted their lives to serving God in song for this generation of children. Yet, I write for those readers who have a genuine thirst for biblical direction on the question of alternative Christian musical forms.

WHAT DOES GOD'S FAVORITE MUSIC SOUND LIKE?

It was one of those phone conversations that I don't particularly enjoy receiving. The caller wanted to "discuss" my position on "so-called contemporary Christian music." Taking a deep breath, I assured him I would be happy to hear his concerns. His idea of a discussion resembled more of a crusade against the evils of Christian rock. After twenty minutes of nonstop harangue, he announced that he was sending me a tape series and study guide called "Striving for Excellence—How to Evaluate Music."[1] I promised to read through and listen to the material when it arrived.

Now, I want you to know that even though I have deep convictions about the positive role of contemporary Christian music, I sincerely invited the Lord's guidance to show me if my beliefs on the subject were off base. With an open mind I listened to the tapes and read through all of the printed material on the evening I received it. Was it possible that I was wrong all of these years? I must admit, the material he sent me had to be the most oppressive approach to music I've ever been asked to analyze. Yet I was willing to consider that they may just be right. But, were they? The answer came the next morning while I was shaving.

The window in my bathroom was open, allowing the morning light and the fresh scent of the day to fill the room. As I shaved, I heard a most unusual sound—the sound of several birds exchanging their morning song in my backyard. And then it struck me—didn't these poor birds (whippoorwills, to be exact) realize that the special melody God placed in their little bodies violated the principles of appropriate music structure as defined by the booklet I just read? I had to smile with joy that the Creator isn't limited to our particular taste in music.

Two weeks later, the phone rang again: "So, Mr. DeMoss, what did you think of the information I mailed you?" I politely shared my bird encounter with him and explained that this is one subject on which we'd have to agree to disagree. I didn't have the heart to tell him that the

---

"I've watched a small portion of Christendom spread rumors about, even outright hatred for, Christian musicians who have devoted their lives to serving God in song for this generation of children."

---

information he sent me was riddled with grave academic errors. For instance, the authors failed to provide *any* documentation for *any* of the sources of information they presented. On a number of occasions they did cite a study conducted by a "certain doctor" or by a "well-known newspaper, such as the *Los Angeles Times*," yet they failed to provide any footnotes or end notes to document these citations. The reader is simply expected to take their word for the validity of what was quoted and trust that the quotation was not taken out of context.

Nor did I explain that the approach to music in "Striving for Excellence" operated on the extremely dangerous and faulty assumption that the only music acceptable to God—indeed, that could be remotely considered as holy—is music created by European and Western civilization. After a fairly good overview of basic music theory, the authors began to inject their own values—the values of Western music theory—into the definition of what makes a "good melody" as well as what are acceptable harmonies for this melody. Their study didn't allow room for the music created by those of Middle Eastern descent (Jesus' culture), Russian, Oriental, nor the sounds of South American cultures—or whippoorwills for that matter.

IN SEARCH OF DEMON BEATS

Over the years I've heard just about every possible argument why rock music is "of the devil," and why Christians cannot use rock music to express themselves—until last week. Last week I met a woman who exclaimed, "Did you know that there is a study that proves if you play rock music to cows, the cows will not be able to give milk at the same rate as they do when you play classical music?"

I'll keep that in mind the next time I'm milking cows.

Then there's the argument that demons dance to the various beat patterns of rock music—"studies" on African music supposedly prove this. (Why pick on African culture? How about Mexican or German music?) Further, there are those who insist that plants prefer classical over rock music. Others aren't playing music to cows and plants; they're studying the effect of rock music on earthworms! Seriously.

Frankly, it's draining to discuss the alleged studies that "prove" the aforementioned effects of rock music on cows, plants, and earthworms. Guess what? The issue is not whether worms give their hearts to Christ. Most of us do care, however, about our teenagers and want them to listen to music that will enhance their walk with the Lord. Though I am aware of thousands of decisions for Jesus through the gift of Christian music, some parents remain apprehensive.

If we are truly interested in answering the question regarding the validity of Christians using rock music in any of its forms (be it pop/rock, folk/rock, soft/rock, hard/rock, jazz/rock, alternative/rock, rock-a-billy/rock, country/rock, heavy metal/rock, rap/rock, or plain ol' rock/rock—whatever that may be), we should dispel and address the misinformation and legitimate concerns surrounding the subject. If I were to boil down all of the concerns that adults have raised with me on this subject over the years, I'd note these five basic issues:

1. Rock music is Satan's music. It's *so* corrupt, it can serve no godly purpose.

2. Contemporary Christian music sounds too worldly.

3. The lyrics are hard to hear, and Christian musicians don't deal with serious issues anyway.

4. Contemporary Christian musicians are only in it for the money.

5. Christian music should be used exclusively to sing praises to the Lord.

WHOSE MUSIC IS IT, ANYWAY?

To those who believe that rock music in its various forms is intrinsically Satan's music and that it cannot be used for godly purposes, let me say at the outset that I don't blame you for thinking that way. After all, many non-Christian musicians, whether they know it or not, have allowed Satan to work through their talent for evil purposes (their talent, incidentally, was a gift from God). There's no doubt that Satan *has* corrupted rock music; chapter 4 makes that painfully clear. But let's not forget that he has also corrupted *all* music, including country western, classical, and opera.

Herein lies the key. Throughout time, there's been (and will continue to be until the Lord returns) a spiritual tension in the cosmos. As God creates, Satan works overtime to corrupt. God is the Author of all creation—the arts and music included. Satan does not have the power to create anything, but he *is* the master of corruption. Even though critics of CCM may comprehend this knowledge, some still contend: "How can God take something as bankrupt as rock music and use it to bring praises to His name?" That's a fair question. It's also a question that could be asked of you and me: how can God use people as evil as we were before we knew Him for His kingdom agenda?

How? It's called *redemption*. When Adam and Eve fell from grace in the Garden of Eden, all of the created order fell with them. When the second Adam, Jesus Christ, came and died on the Cross, He paid the price to redeem all of creation from the decay and death that was set in motion by our first parents. His finished work on the Cross enabled the process of redemption. God takes sinful, reprobate, and morally depraved people like you and me, and He transforms us into His children. He can do that because He paid the price necessary to redeem us from death. Then, if that weren't enough of a miracle, He uses us as His disciples to teach others about salvation and eternal life.

In like fashion, God has paid the price and has the power to redeem all music for His purposes.

Why Should the Devil Have All the Good Music?

Here's an interesting story about a young, God-fearing teenager. Raised in a good home, this boy had some rather exceptional musical talents. The only problem was his boredom with the music played at church. He probably wondered why the devil had such interesting music to offer, when his church seemed to specialize in antiquated styles. Worn out by constant complaining, his father decided to challenge him to write his own hymns. The year was 1690; the boy—Isaac Watts. Responding to his dad's prompting, Watts ultimately penned more than three hundred fifty hymns. Among them were "When I Survey the Wondrous Cross," "Joy to the World," and "O God, Our Help in Ages Past."

Martin Luther's story is also worth mentioning. Frustrated with the church music of his day, Luther was known to borrow the melodies from a few favorite German drinking tunes, while replacing the lyrics with his new Christian verses. No wonder some leaders of the church back then had a problem with "A Mighty Fortress Is Our God"—the music was originally a drinking melody!

A gifted musician in his own right, Dana Key (lead vocalist and guitarist for Degarmo and Key) did some homework on the history of Christian music and found that "many of our greatest hymn writers have used the popular, secular music of their day for their hymn lyrics. Bernard of Clairvaux, a twelfth-century Christian, set the words of 'O Sacred Head Now Wounded' to the tune of a German jig."[2] Digging deeper, Key discovered, "Apparently, the writer of many of the Psalms did the same thing. Look at the instructions before Psalm 56 (To the tune of 'A Dove on Distant Oaks') and Psalms 57, 58, and 59 (To the tune of 'Do Not Destroy'). These instructions to the 'song leader' of the day tell him which current tune serves as good accompaniment for this psalm."[3]

The second issue still troubling the church centuries after Bernard, Watts, and Luther is the matter of Christian music which "sounds like the world." Christian musicians today, as it was then, are charged with *guilt by association*. If secular rock music is riddled with evil, then Christian rock will likewise be evil.

Whenever I'm asked how God could use something that resembles current styles in music for His glory, I bring up the matter of trains—trains during Nazi Germany to be exact. During that dark period of world history, trains were used to ship millions of Jews to concentration

"Christian musicians today . . . are charged with guilt by association. If secular rock music is riddled with evil, then Christian rock will likewise be evil."

camps for hard labor or extermination. Almost daily, trains would depart various rail stations throughout Germany packed with humans for the holocaust. Trains were so important to Hitler's war machine, I can understand how some could view all trains as intrinsically evil.

After the war, these same trains would be used for good purposes—to help rebuild the war-torn region. Here's the point: the trains did not have any choice in how they were used. They could be used for humanitarian purposes or in the destruction of millions. Trains are amoral objects, without any inherent moral attributes. The same is true of music. Music is made up of individual notes, chords, and rhythmic patterns that can be played by a few or many different instruments. The notes do not have a choice in the matter. It is the musician who determines how the musical creation will be used—whether it will be for good or evil. Even if the majority of trains or songs were used by man for evil, that doesn't alter the fact that they can also be put to good uses.

Now, if I had been shipped to a Nazi prison camp on a train, I'd probably never be able to ride a train the rest of my life for fear of the horrible memories such a trip would produce. But that doesn't preclude others from enjoying a train ride. And so it is with music. For those who have participated in the more negative aspects of the secular music scene, it's understandable that they might not be able to appreciate Christian music if it reminds them of their past. However, this individual shouldn't impose his negative association of music onto the rest of the body of Christ.

What's That They're Saying?

A third criticism of contemporary Christian music that parents have expressed to me is how difficult the words are to hear; and when you can make them out, some parents claim they're not dealing with anything of significance. Like cotton candy, it's all sugar-coated fluff. Several things may account for the difficulty we adults may have with picking out the words. First, we're getting older and our hearing isn't what it used to be. I know that my left ear picks up sound better than my right. The older I become, chances are both ears will need a touch of assistance to do their job. A grandparent will have a different opinion than that of a twelve-year-old if asked what a proper lyrical balance should sound like.

Second, we adults don't have the time or patience to really pay attention to what a singer is communicating, especially those rapid-rhyming, fast-talking rap artists. A child has more time on his hands to spend listening to music as a *primary* activity. Through repetition, he becomes familiar with what the artist is singing. Adults are different. Many of us use music as a *secondary,* background experience. For us, if the words don't absolutely jump out of the speakers and hit us on the head, we'll miss them.

A third reason some become critical of the difficulty of hearing the words stems from a poor sound system at a concert they've attended. Any professional sound management group can attest to the fact that the job of providing sound reinforcement in a concert hall is tricky business at best. Some halls are naturally more ambient than others. The reverberation of sound in those halls wreaks havoc on a good, balanced audio mix. Then there are what are known as dead spots—areas of a hall where the sound level drops significantly. If you're sitting in one of those areas, you'll have a difficult time understanding much of anything.

Whatever the reason for our inability to occasionally pick out the lyrics, virtually every Christian artist that I've examined prints his or her lyrics inside the jacket of the recorded product. By contrast, my experience with thousands of secular artists would place those who print lyrics at a mere 40 percent. Without a doubt, Christian artists on the whole desire their listener to get the message. Many will mention the scriptural passages that inspired their writing.

How about the accusations that all Christian music is sugar-coated fluff. Is that assessment accurate? One adult made this generalization based on a tape by a sister duo called Heather and Kirsten. Actually, the lyrics on this tape *were* rather elementary. Mind you, the girls who were singing were only twelve and fourteen years old. (At that age, it's a bit much to expect anything too heavy.)

Admittedly, from time to time there are musicians who are young in the Lord and who write rather basic material. That's okay. There will be listeners who are young in the Lord who can benefit from a review of

---

> *"You'll find Christian musicians have the courage to tackle virtually all aspects of our existence—abortion, infidelity, the homeless, suicide, gang warfare, salvation, sexual purity; just about any subject you could identify is addressed from a Christian framework."*

---

the first steps of the Christian faith. Don't get me wrong. I *have* run across some pretty lame material. There are always a few folks who insist that "God gave me this song." One listen and I'm tempted to ask, "But did He tell you to share it with anyone?"—it's that awful.

Yet, to insist that all contemporary Christian musicians write rudimentary material, based upon a few who do, is simply unfair. You'll find Christian musicians have the courage to tackle virtually all aspects of our existence—abortion, infidelity, the homeless, suicide, gang warfare, salvation, sexual purity; just about any subject you could identify is addressed from a Christian framework. And some artists like Petra and Degarmo and Key have provided the listener with a complete study guide to dig deeper into the topics they've examined in their songs.

Money Matters

Another common charge leveled against musicians who seek to minister through music is that they're only in it for the *money*. Antagonists argue that the music these musicians make can't be valid because they've created it for the wrong reasons. During 1991, with the newfound success for Amy Grant and Michael W. Smith on the secular pop charts, these accusations have been stirred up again.

Several perspectives are worth our consideration. First, the notion that *all* Christian musicians are in it for the money is ludicrous. How can I be so sure? For several years I was a promoter of Christian concerts in Philadelphia and had the opportunity to work with a wide range of musicians. I remember Marty McCall (then with a band called Fireworks) showing up at the concert hall in a beat-up, tired-out, and very old mobile home. A second car dragged the band's equipment in a U-haul-type trailer, which appeared to be on its last leg. They drove fourteen hours from Tennessee for a concert in Pennsylvania for about six hundred people. Hardly the big time!

Working with Marty that evening I learned what a compassionate man of God he was—a man deeply burdened for the teens in the audience. The guys in the band hung around for quite some time sharing one-on-one with dozens of teenagers who had questions about the Christian faith. I could share similar stories from concerts that I sponsored with the Degarmo and Key band, GLAD, James Ward, Amy Grant, Servant, Joe English, Andrus Blackwood and Company, and several other artists who are no longer in business because they couldn't afford to pay their bills.

Speaking of bills, my partner and I invested and lost more than fifty thousand dollars over a two-year period promoting Christian music. Many weeks I'd go without a full salary just to keep the office open. Frankly, I'd do it again to witness the impact we had on so many teens who were searching for a relevant musical expression for their faith.

Another perspective worth considering is the matter of making money in the first place. Many passages of Scripture speak in praise of hard work and the rewards that accompany those who are faithful in their calling. First Timothy 5:18 makes it clear that "The laborer is worthy of his wages." In fact, in verse 17 Paul takes it a step further and suggests a "double honor" for those who work hard at preaching and teaching the Word of God. So, then, why are we critical of Christian musicians who attempt to earn a decent wage from their ministry through music? Furthermore, why aren't critics of Christian musicians tackling Christian lawyers, accountants, computer programmers, and doctors who may be making six-figure incomes? It seems that these discussions about finances are disingenuous.

Sing Your Praises—and Blues—to the Lord

The fifth argument frequently leveled against contemporary Christian music occurs when the musician decides to sing something other than a praise chorus. Some detractors feel that praise and worship music is the only fitting subject for Christian song. On the surface, who could argue with the priorities of praise and worship? However, the Hebrews of Old Testament times provide us with a different, and usually overlooked, vantage point.

For them, worship was a way of life, not an activity confined to services held on the Sabbath. Thus, the music they used related to a wide variety of daily activities. The Scriptures picture them using song in many ways—from a celebration of love to moments of intense loneliness, from unforgettable happiness to unimaginable helplessness. The following is a partial listing of functions in which music was employed by the Hebrews, clearly demonstrating the diversity of song used by God's chosen people:

- Music accompanied leave-taking with guests (Genesis 31:27).
- Music signaled triumph over the nation's enemies (Exodus 15:19–21).
- Music welcomed conquerors returning home from victory (Judges 11:32–34).
- Music was used to quiet the troubled soul (1 Samuel 16:15–17).
- Music celebrated the king's marriage (Psalm 45).
- Music enhanced the joys of sex within marriage (The Song of Solomon).
- Music accompanied King David's anger at God's apparent lack of response (Psalm 13).
- Music was used in what was the equivalence of singing "the blues" (Psalm 42:3–6).
- Music assisted the cry for help and deliverance from oppression (Psalm 59:1–5).
- Music was used to thank God for His justice (Psalm 9).

To limit music for purposes of worship only, as some would have it, is to rob the believer of his tool for the expression of emotional, physical, or spiritual needs. Whether it's the blues or a mountaintop experience that you'd like to verbalize, these Scriptures demonstrate that God delights to hear His people express themselves honestly through song.

HELP TEENS CHANGE THEIR "TUNES"

Her eyes were filled with tears as she stood holding on to her husband's arm. I don't recall her name, but I haven't forgotten what she said. "Bob, never again will I challenge my children about the contemporary Christian music they want to purchase!" She explained, "After I saw tonight's program and understood what my youngsters are up against in this culture, how could I deny them the positive influence of Christian music?"

When it comes to antisocial, ungodly messages in the music and the entertainment children consume, it's easy to know what we're *against*. But what are we *for*? What options can we offer them? This concerned mother had just sat through one of the "A Generation at Risk" seminars that I conduct for Focus on the Family. Her eyes were opened to the incredible assault upon her adolescents, and she knew that simply "cursing the darkness" was not enough. She came to understand that the task of discipling her children needed to include lighting a candle of hope— providing positive musical alternatives.

I am painfully aware that some Christian teens live in homes where most forms of Christian music outside of traditional hymns are frowned upon. Many of the more than two thousand letters I've received from junior highers express utter frustration with their parents because their folks are not supportive of the positive lyrics in Christian music.

Leslie from Chattanooga, Tennessee, wrote: "I love God very much, but I have been listening to a lot of junk. Since reading your column in *Brio* magazine, I've switched to Christian music. The problem is that my parents seem more upset about Christian music than the junk I *was* listening to. How can I help them understand the real difference Christian music is making in my life?" And Ray from Wallula, Washington, explains that there is a difference of opinion between his parents: "My mom thinks Christian music is great, but my dad thinks it's as bad or worse than secular rock." The net result? This youngster is not permitted to plug into life-enriching music.

Perhaps you've been suspicious about music that makes the foot tap. My prayer is that the things we've considered in this chapter has shed new light on the issues you've been wrestling with over this subject. Let me add one more thing to consider. In Matthew 12:43–45 Jesus describes what will take place if you cast off the unclean spirit and don't fill the void. If we ask our youngsters to clean up their tape players, we should be willing to provide them with appropriate alternatives. To this day, I am grateful that my parents did just that.[4]

The next time you go shopping, consider stopping by a local Christian book and tape store. Many have a listening center where you can get an idea of the options that are available to teens. Let me give you one helpful tip: if your kids are into Motley Crüe, Megadeth, and Slayer, Sandi Patti is not the right choice! Boy, can she sing, but there are others who may make a better match with what your teens enjoy.

DANCING IN THE SPIRIT

How, then, should a discerning person approach Christian music? The same way he approaches all aspects of his life—seeking the Lord's wisdom and guidance. Psalms 149 and 150, for example, encourage the believer to do three things as he praises the Lord: shout, make a joyful *noise,* and, yes, dance. To dance implies the use of rhythm—a beat, in other words. To make noise requires fullness of sound and plenty of volume. As for shouting, well, that's a tough requirement to satisfy in most church environments these days. So, if I were to ask you what style of music would be most conducive to fulfilling the scriptural mandate of Psalms 149 and 150, what style would you select? Hymns? Folk? Classical? Rock?

Objectively speaking, rock music offers a bountiful supply of possibilities for shouting, noise, and dancing. Without taking anything away from the hymns (because I happen to have many favorites since childhood), most hymns do not lend themselves to anything more rigorous than perhaps a slow dance. By the way, as long as we're on the subject, let me confess that I've never been a good dancer; I'm probably as graceful as a bull in a china shop. Come to think of it, a slow dance is about all that I can handle without total personal embarrassment. But don't let me stand in the way of a child who wants to dance as King David danced—*as unto the Lord.*

While we are free in Christ to enjoy music that lifts our souls, we still must test the spirits. Even Christian musicians, pastors, religious educators, parents, and others whom we may admire, can stray from the straight and narrow. We're all imperfect human beings. From time to time, humans make mistakes or exercise poor judgment. The process of learning to discern which we've studied through this book, when applied to Christian entertainment, empowers us to confidently make the best choices.

I realize that questions over the role of Christian music in your home may still be lingering in your mind. For obvious reasons, one chapter cannot possibly cover all of the ground surrounding this dynamic topic. As a footnote to our discussion, let me point you to two excellent books (available from your local bookstore) that examine contemporary Christian music more closely: *Today's Music: A Window to Your Child's Soul* (Elgin, IL: David C. Cook Publishing Co., 1990) by Al Menconi and *Don't Stop the Music* (Grand Rapids, MI: Zondervan, 1989) by Dana Key.

PERSONALLY SPEAKING

After reviewing a rough draft of this manuscript, my mom and dad thought that an important part of this discussion was missing—the role of Christian music in my own life. Since my parents know best, I decided to sit down and reflect on my junior and senior high school years. As I looked back, I began to remember the incredible feeling of excitement whenever I discovered a new Christian artist. You see, back in 1973, very few musicians were recording "Jesus music." There were, of course, a few independent record projects by little-known regional artists—musicians who were typically associated with Campus Crusade, Inter-Varsity, and the like. A good start, but nothing like the incredible choices teens have today.

Like a sponge, I would soak up anything and everything that looked promising. (Boy, did I bump into a few disappointments!) I tracked down any and all new leads. I recall riding in my cousin Harry Constantine's Cougar when he popped in an eight-track tape by a guy named Paul Clark. I couldn't believe my ears! This was great music, and he was singing about the Lord with instruments I enjoyed. We drove all over Chicago that very afternoon trying to find a bookstore that carried his albums.

Before long I amassed a small museum of Jesus music. Needing a place to store and listen to all these records, my parents permitted me to build a recording studio in the basement of our home—carpet on the walls and all! Downstairs in my studio, I'd bring both saved and un-

---

> ***"While we are free in Christ to enjoy
> music that lifts our souls, we still
> must test the spirits."***

---

saved friends to listen to this new music I was discovering. Often, while driving friends around in my 1968 Monaco, I'd slap a Christian tape into the deck, which, of course, my friends had never heard. I didn't tell them it was Jesus music. Curious about what we were listening to, they'd ask who was the new group. I, of course, played it up as if this was some hot new release from the underground circuit! It always worked—"Where can I get it?" They were hooked.

Who were the musicians that had a significant impact upon my life during my high school and college years? Although this is not a complete listing, you'll get the picture. I've also indicated which of their albums had the greatest influence on my life, which might not be their most recent project. Many of these titles are out of print today, so you'll just have to come to my studio and listen with me! Stylistically, these artists span a wide range of folk music to some heavier sounds. In alphabetical order they are:

- Jonathan and Charles (*Another Week to Go*)
- Paul Clark and Friends (*Songs for the Savior Vol. 2*)
- Andrea Crouch and the Disciples (*Live*)
- Fireworks (*Live Fireworks*)
- John Fisher (*Simple Pleasures*)
- GLAD (*Beyond a Star*)
- Keith Green (*No Compromise*)
- Mark Heard (*Stop the Dominos*)
- Honeytree (*Honeytree*)
- Phil Keaggy (*What a Day*)

- Degarmo and Key (*This Ain't Hollywood*)
- Larry Norman (*Only Visiting This Planet*)
- Michael Omartian (*White Horse*)
- Petra (*Never Say Die*)
- New Song (*Born Twice*)
- Randy Stonehill (*The Sky Is Falling*)
- The Resurrection Band (*Awaiting Your Reply*)
- James Ward (*Himself*)

Now that I'm older, the list contains a few new faces alongside of the old. They are:

- Bob Bennett (*Lord of the Past*)
- The Altar Boys (*Forever Mercy*)
- Steve Camp (*Fire and Ice*)
- The Choir (*Diamonds and Rain*)
- Ric Cua (*Can't Stand Too Tall*)
- Idle Cure (*2nd Avenue*)
- Dion (*Inside Job*)
- Kim Hill (*Talk About Life*)
- Phil Keaggy (*Find Me in These Fields*)
- Degarmo and Key (*D&K*)
- Kings X (*Out of the Silent Planet*)
- Kerry Livgren (*Seeds of Change*)
- Mastedon (*Lofcaudio*)
- Charlie Peacock (*The Secret of Time*)
- Petra (*Beyond Belief*)
- Leslie Phillips (*Black and White in a Grey World*)
- Say-so (*Say-so*)
- Mansfield/Turner (*Blues with a Feelin'*)
- James Ward (*More Piano, Please*)
- Matthew Ward (*Fortress*)
- The Winans (*Return*)

To each of these artists I owe a special word of thanks. They'll never know the vital role they played during my formative years through their gift of music. Even now, I thank them for enriching my life with their incredible talent and their faithfulness to the Lord. And I praise God for parents who provided a home environment that encouraged our involvement in Christian music. Thanks to these musicians and my caring parents, I'll be dancing to the beat of a different drummer throughout my lifetime.

8

QUESTIONS AND ANSWERS

*A*lthough I've attempted to answer many commonly asked questions thus far, a number of tough issues have yet to be addressed. Don't be surprised if several of the concerns sound painfully familiar; these are actual questions raised by parents around the country with whom I've spoken. Isn't it good to know that other families are wrestling with similar matters!

Question: Our local theater has eight movie screens. On one hand, it's great to have so many options when we go to the theater. On the other hand, the management is sloppy in its enforcement of NC-17 films. In fact, they don't make any attempt to enforce the "no children under seventeen permitted" rating. Several times I've seen young, unsupervised kids walk right into a movie rated NC-17. Do we have any legal recourse?

Answer: American families owe a special thanks to Jack Valenti, president of the Motion Picture Association of America for giving us something to do with our free time. Jack knew that we parents were beginning to get bored with the day-to-day responsibilities of raising a family.

To help us spend our free time, Jack changed the rules of the movie rating game to include the new category: NC-17 (no children under seventeen permitted). Here's how the game works. Producers of X-rated fare have their pornographic films reclassified to the less threatening sounding NC-17. In turn, theater owners around the country feel better about booking porno movies in their "family" multiplex cinemas.

Enter the children. "Hi, I'd like a ticket to see *Dick Tracy*." No problem. Junior can buy a ticket to see this movie, but the clever child wanders into any film playing at his multiplex cinema, including those rated NC-17. Here's where the fun begins. Somehow it's our job to make sure that kids don't play the revolving door game when they go to see a movie.

How we achieve that goal is our problem. We can't count on the theater owners to pay for security guards at the door to NC-17 films, and we can't take them to court when children do get in. This, of course, is because the rating system is only a *suggestion,* not the law. There are no legal teeth to "no children under 17 permitted." It's just a guideline.

So, once again, thanks, Jack, for giving us this new game, even if it was something we consumers didn't ask for and even if it's a game that we're virtually guaranteed to lose.

Although I'm being a bit sarcastic, in truth, by adding the new category Jack Valenti scored big points with the film industry while disregarding the problem he created for American families who have better things to do than play policeman at the community cinema. Since you cannot apply legal pressure to the theater management, begin by writing a letter of concern to the owner. First, encourage him to stop carrying NC-17 rated films, citing the problems we've discussed. Next, if he won't consider dropping NC-17 titles, ask him to outline what, if any, steps he will take to keep minors from viewing these shows in the future. Allow him several weeks to respond.

If you don't hear back or you are dissatisfied with his answer, consider "going public" with your concern. Describe your behind-the-scenes efforts to resolve this problem in an editorial in the local newspaper. Depending on how aggressive you want to be, you may consider sharing your concern with local PTA, church, and civic groups. Calling for a boycott of all movies at that theater, regardless of the rating, will bring economic pressure to bear. Although picketing is a lot of work to coordinate, it can be an effective tool to consider.

Question: My child has been after me to buy him a Sony Walkman-type portable tape player with headphones. A lot of his friends have one, but I'm not sure it's a good idea. What would you recommend?

Answer: As a society, we manage to play music virtually everywhere—in the car, waiting at the doctor's or dentist's office, standing in line at the grocery store, or relaxing at the restaurant. Music is inescapable. Department store executives have learned the secret of keeping shoppers shopping—play "feel good" Muzak (that nondescript programmed variety). I've been in many hotels that piped music into their elevators. Heaven forbid that I be alone with my thoughts while traveling up three floors!

> *"The problem with Walkman-type players is not their portability. Rather, it's with the headphones. . . . Your child has created a private world that only he can experience—one that excludes his parents."*

Jogging and bike riding were two places that music had not penetrated—that is, not until the advent of the Walkman. Leave it to Sony to revolutionize the way we exercise. Now we *can* take it with us, and millions of Americans do. Don't laugh, but since the development of the mini-portable tape player, several companies have marketed waterproof sets that some teens actually use in the shower! Although much could be said philosophically about our dependency on perpetual audio distraction and the inability to be content while alone with our thoughts, that wasn't the focus of your question.

As I see it, the problem with Walkman-type players is not their portability. Rather, it's with the headphones. Safety considerations while wearing headphones is a genuine concern. Walkers, joggers, and bike riders cannot hear the sound of oncoming cars. Nor can they anticipate the footsteps of a would-be assailant. This aside, there's no debate that their usage keeps the overall noise level down in the home—a real plus for you. But at what cost? Your child has created a private world that only he can experience—one that excludes his parents. On the contrary, you *want* to listen to what they are hearing.

I'd suggest a two-tiered approach. First, keep headphones off-limits for children through their junior high years—through the ninth grade. One ploy to waylay potential hostility at this mandate would be to offer them assistance so that they can buy a decent stereo or portable tape player with speakers. Your goal through these formative years will be to instill in them a love for the best in music by listening together as a family. One great way to help them establish good habits would be to teach them that prayer we discussed in chapter 5: "Help me to love what You love and hate what You hate."

The second tier: allow high-school-aged youth to purchase a headset. Remind them that they still must uphold the family standard (see also chapter 5). Explain that you are trusting them to use their best judgment in the music they will be selecting. And, reserve the right to pull the plug if they begin to spend too much time by themselves apart from the family routine.

Extended isolation is to be avoided. On the other hand, part of being a teenager is to be at a stage in life when pulling away from the folks to establish their individuality is a natural step before leaving the nest. Some privacy and isolation is permissible. You can keep the balance by spending plenty of "nose to nose" time throughout their adolescent years.

Question: I try to set a standard and encourage the family to make good entertainment choices. Unfortunately, my husband is not particularly supportive. He doesn't think there's a problem with allowing our kids to listen to what they want or to watch whatever they like on the video player. How can I gain his support?

Answer: There are two primary reasons why some spouses shirk this responsibility. First, they don't understand how warped the entertainment landscape has become in recent years. The common reaction of the "live and let live" parenting approach goes something like this: "Give me a break; I survived the sixties with all of its permissiveness and drug experimentation. Things can't be any worse than that—and I turned out okay."

If your spouse were to read the first few chapters of this book, he'd see how wrong the assertion—that things can't be any worse—really is. And that's precisely the point. He is undereducated on these matters and suffers from the first denial—a denial of any problem. Several suggestions come to mind. Obtain a copy of the video *Rising to the Challenge* by the Parents' Music Resource Center. On the subject of contemporary music, this is a real eye-opener! (Write: Video Offer, PMRC, 1500 Arlington Blvd., Suite 130, Arlington, VA 22209 or call 703–527–9466.)

Second, you might consider subscribing to *Parental Guidance,* a newsletter produced by Focus on the Family. Each month it provides you with timely information on a score of musicians—the good, the bad,

---

> **"When someone's heart is not sensitive to the things of the Lord, it will be less offended by the slick suburban smut that Hollywood serves us day after day."**

---

and the ugly. (Write: Focus on the Family, Colorado Springs, CO 80995 or call 719–531–3400.) Let him look at a few issues. With time, he'll come to see that the problem is bigger than he may have assumed.

The second reason your spouse is shirking his responsibility could be due to a heart condition. When someone's heart is not sensitive to the things of the Lord, it will be less offended by the slick suburban smut that Hollywood serves us day after day. Frankly, it will take a lot more than a videotape or this book to turn him around. Your best bet is to commit him to prayer on a regular basis. Pray that he becomes the man of God, the spiritual leader that God intended. You might want to solicit the help of a prayer partner. True, it would be great to have his support as you work on the matter of appropriate entertainment for your home. But that should come naturally when he's cultivated a deeper love for the Lord.

One suggestion: if you decide to ask him to be compliant on the matter of a family entertainment standard (before his heart is right), time your discussion when the children are not present and avoid confrontational, "holier-than-thou" tones.

Question: On two occasions I've allowed my eight-year-old to go to a friend's house for a sleep-over party. Both times the parents of that home permitted the youngsters to rent some movies which, in my estimation, were highly inappropriate for the kids. How can I ensure this doesn't happen again and still allow my son to maintain social contacts?

Answer: Staying up all night, telling stories, laughing, and wrestling till you're so tired even the floor feels comfortable—truly, there's nothing quite like sleeping at a friend's home when you're a kid. Actually, looking back at my childhood, I enjoyed having classmates over at our home more than I desired to stay at their house—probably because my mom made a better lunch for us to take to school the next day! For obvious reasons, hosting the overnight at your place provides you with the advantage in controlling their activities. I'd urge you to consider opening your home on a regular basis for your children's friends. Before rolling your eyes at the thought of more housework preparing to entertain someone else's little monster, it doesn't have to be that much more work for you. My folks allowed me to have friends over almost every week. The deal was an exchange: I would clean the bathrooms and vacuum the house!

If a visit to his friend's makes more sense, or if you just need a quiet respite from the action, call the other child's parent and ask him to respect your desire to protect young eyes from mind pollution. You might also send along an especially fun game for the kids to play as an alternative to their vegging in front of the tube until their eyes dry out!

Question: I am a divorced mother with three children. When the children are with me, I make sure that we carefully select good TV shows to watch. If we have the money to rent a movie, I'm pretty picky about what we'll tolerate. Overall, I think I'm doing an okay job. But the problem is when the kids are with their father. Not only is he unsupportive of these efforts, he's even hostile to them. Is there any way I can control their media diet when they are at his home?

Answer: My guess is that any attempt to control the media consumption in his home will fail miserably. Furthermore, you're walking a delicate line because you should avoid bad-mouthing the ex-spouse to the children. Instead, try this "back door" approach. First, befriend a couple whose marriage you respect. Arrange to have them over for dinner. Before they arrive, explain that your kids would greatly benefit to see a father who shares your high standards. The objective is to let them see that not all daddies have permissive entertainment standards.

You may want to have them over on several occasions before attempting to cover too much ground. This would provide time for familiarity and trust to be developed between the couple and your youngsters. Some of the most profound influences in a child's life are heroes other than their parents. Take courage! You don't have to go it alone. God can use the example of another couple to help share your burden.

Question: Our junior higher announced that her school will be hosting a dance next month. What concerns me is that the music the disc jockey has played in the past was at times highly sexual and inappropriate for young teens. What, if anything, can I do? I remember going to a school dance when I was a teen so I'm not totally against her going.

Answer: I used to be a disc jockey who played music for dances and weddings. Personally, my goal was to play only songs that contained a morally positive message—I even threw in a few Christian tunes for the fun of it. You could say the dances I dee-jayed were "Prince, Motley Crüe, and Madonna-free music marathons!" These, and many other popular artists, never saw the strobe of my turntables. But the kids had a blast. Based on experience, I know it *is* possible to sponsor a great dance without stepping on the feet of moral principles.

If there isn't a disc jockey in your area who has a similar approach, ask to have the song list and lyrics submitted in advance. The dance committee, which should include a few adults, could then screen the listing for inappropriate selections. I know of a number of schools who have taken this approach with real success. If the DJ wants your future business, he'll respect this process. In a few instances, the school may not be cooperative. In these situations, you might consider sponsoring an alternative dance or function.

Question: My children ride the school bus every day. It's a thirty-minute ride, so the bus driver allows the kids to play tapes on their portable "boom" boxes on the way. Most of the time the music, from what my children have told me, is okay. But on a number of occasions they've come home virtually in tears over the lyrics which they heard. They've asked the other kids to turn it down, but they were ridiculed for doing so. I don't think it's right that my

children are subjected to degrading lyrics on the public school bus. What can be done?

Answer: A college professor told me that once, while he was shaving in the morning, his little six-year-old boy went strolling past the bathroom singing a rousing chorus of "Do you think I'm sexy—and you want my body." Having regained his composure after nearly cutting his face, my professor quizzed his son on where he picked up those lyrics. It's amazing what kids learn on the bus on the way to school.

I still recall being approached by a lady in the St. Louis area after I finished speaking at a seminar. She had the biggest smile on her face as she described the exact problem you've mentioned, but with one difference. Hers was a success story. She said, "Bob, I just knew that the school board had no idea what was in some of the music." Patiently, in nonalarmist tones she presented her concern. Documenting specific examples with a set of typed lyrics was invaluable. And they agreed with her! The public playing of music on the bus ended immediately. What's more, the next school year the new policy was still in effect.

I would like to add a note here. Personally, I think it is regrettable that we have to restrict music on school buses. I am not a killjoy who has nothing better to do than make life miserable for adolescents. Many bands are releasing positive, thought-provoking material worthy of public enjoyment. However, those musicians who routinely exploit sex, substance abuse, violence, or who dwell on other antisocial themes have ruined it for everyone else.

Question: We live in an area that has poor television reception, so most families have cable service. We debated the matter for a long while, but my wife and I finally agreed to get the basic cable package. After our house was wired, I noticed that Music Television (MTV) came with the other channels. It didn't take long for us to agree we didn't want MTV playing in our home. Since it's a part of the package deal, is there any way we can dispense with it?

Answer: When I used to live in Pittsburgh, there was a huge billboard on the way to work that boasted "Cable TV Is Good for You." Hmm. I guess the next thing they'll expect us to believe is that "three out of four doctors prefer cable TV"!

Since many families don't share this wishful thinking, some cities have a stipulation in their contract with the cable company requiring them to provide blocking of unwanted channels, including Music Television, usually at no extra charge to the consumer. A quick call to your local cable customer service line will resolve that question. If their technology does not allow them to block this service prior to sending it to your home, explore the option of a "lock box" or similar access-restricting device in the home.

You could also ask the city council to require the cable company to provide MTV blocking the next time their contract is up for renewal.

Question: When our school loosened its dress code, permitting students greater latitude in their campus garb, it wasn't long before wearing a T-shirt was the popular thing to do—particularly shirts sporting various music groups. My wife and I refuse to allow our children to own T-shirts by certain offensive bands. Our kids insist that because they are not into the music—that they only like the art design—we should permit them to wear the shirts. How do I handle this one?

Answer: Sometimes teens forget that they become a "walking billboard" for the musicians that they plaster on their bodies, even if they are only into the artwork. Let me illustrate. It's not often that I play on the challenge court when I play racquetball, primarily because I am only a slightly better than average player. This particular Saturday, however, I was up for something different and found myself taking the challenge. I had just finished fending off several opponents and was ready to leave when I was approached by a teen who wanted to take me on.

As I sized up my opponent, I couldn't help but notice that he was wearing a T-shirt by the band called Christian Death. Needless to say I didn't feel particularly excited about playing ball with him! For all I knew, he was a nice guy. But my decision not to play ball was based upon a first impression formed primarily by his dress. What we wear does communicate to others.

If your teenagers don't believe that teens notice or care what each other is wearing, have them try this comical situation on for size. My associate Tim Collins and I were standing in line for an Iron Maiden concert. (We were there to do some added research on the band.) We were surrounded by kids with T-shirts representing bands like Slayer, Possessed, Judas Priest, Venom, AC/DC, and others. Here's the twist. As an experiment, before leaving for the concert, I asked Tim to wear a bright, fluorescent pink T-shirt. Painted across the front in bold type read "God Is Awesome!"

You should have heard some of the comments from the fellow concert-goers! One guy next to me whispered to his buddy, "See that kid with the pink shirt? I wonder what *he's* into." There's no doubt that teens are aware of the images on their clothing. I agree with you that to wear clothing with the logo or artwork by certain problematic groups implies endorsement. My mom would encourage us to ask, "Would Jesus wear it?" whenever the subject came up. She was right! Somehow I can't picture Him wearing an AC/DC "I'm on a Highway to Hell" shirt.

You might also point out that when a fan buys a shirt they are economically supporting the group, keeping them in business to produce degrading music. And for bands who have a well-known drug habit, it's your money that enables them to pay for their habit. Take, for example, the mega-group Guns N' Roses. Their first album, *Appetite for Destruction,* sold over twelve million copies. At an average retail price of twelve dollars per copy that one album generated one hundred forty-four million dollars. The band, of course, didn't make all of that, but their share had to be in the millions.

To further their popularity, they released a T-shirt which rock fan magazines called the "Rape Scene." It featured this illustration with the title: "Guns N' Roses was here." No matter how good the artwork (if that is possible), rape is a crime and should be shunned, not paraded on the backs of adolescent boys.

What the band has done with their money is anyone's guess. We do know that several members of the band have had serious addictions to alcohol and drugs. And, thanks to millions of fans, they have all the money they'll ever need to sustain their appetite for self-destruction.

Question: My son is in the ninth grade at a private Christian school. Yesterday, I learned that one of the teachers showed his class *Pretty Woman,* which is rated R. All of the students were underaged. Furthermore, we were not given the option of pulling him from the class prior to its showing. Am I right to be upset by this?

Answer: A real highlight for me as a student was the few times that the teacher would incorporate a film, slides, or in rare instances (due to the limited technology in 1974), a videotape into the class activity. I

"You might also point out that when a fan buys a shirt they are economically supporting the group, keeping them in business to produce degrading music."

---

loved to watch a program and then have the opportunity to discuss or debate. The teaching profession has slowly caught on to the reality that we live in a multimedia-oriented society. Not surprisingly, cable's Nickelodeon channel in October of 1990 launched a commercial-free cable program for use in schools. Using puppetry, animation, music, and humor, they attempt to tackle a wide range of important lessons and world events visually.

Before answering your question, I want to underline the positive usage of various media in the classroom. Used selectively, it can be an important part of the learning process.

Now, is it right for you to be upset about its misuse? Absolutely. Although this is a problem which seems to occur more frequently in public schools, sometimes teachers at private schools make the same mistake. Regardless, no student should be required to watch a film with the inappropriate material typically found in R-rated movies. I'd bring this matter up with both the teacher and the principal. Even if it was an exception, it reflects poor judgment. Incidentally, you're more likely to get a sympathetic hearing if you've previously applauded the teacher and the administration for good things they've done.

Urge the school to notify parents before the showing of feature films in the future, including those rated PG or PG-13, since many contain indecent language and sexual situations. Furthermore, the administration should provide optional activities for those who do not wish to participate.

Question: My daughter went on a church youth retreat for the weekend. When she got home, she mentioned that part of their entertainment was to watch a movie each night. It seems that all of the movies this youth minister brought along were R-rated. We spoke to him about this because we don't believe he used good judgment. After all, this was supposed to be a time for spiritual renewal—not soaking the brain with Hollywood's unhealthy imagery. He dismissed our concerns, stating that we were just too conservative. Furthermore, he told me if we didn't like the programming at youth retreats we should go find another church. How typical is this kind of attitude among youth ministers?

Answer: Actually, it sounds like you bumped into one of the exceptions rather than the rule. Most youth pastors with whom I've had contact are deeply grieved over the trashy movies and music which target teens. Take, for example, the time I went to an AC/DC concert in Pittsburgh with Damon Fogal, a youth pastor. Our objective was to study the concert "mission field." After the show, with ringing ears we followed the band back to its hotel.

In nonconfrontive tones, I watched Damon pour out his heart as he explained to Brian Johnson, lead singer for AC/DC, how their music complicated the efforts of many youth pastors in Pittsburgh. "The reason some folks picket your concerts," he explained, "is because the antisocial, party theme in your songs is counterproductive to the spiritual welfare of teens." As we left, Damon reflected how AC/DC could undo the progress of kids in his youth group—progress made with six months of hard work—in just one night.

Although I haven't taken a formal survey, my experience tells me that the immature attitude held by your youth leader is abnormal. In fact, more often than not, I've heard youth pastors lament that it is the parents who are permissive, even lax, when it comes to the entertainment allowed in the home. They feel unsupported in their efforts to instill proper values about music and movies with the teens they've been asked to disciple.

If in doubt where he stands, in the future discuss with the youth director *prior* to a retreat or church function what plans he may have to include the use of films.

Question: Our son plays the drums. He likes to listen to a variety of styles of music so that he can learn new drumming techniques. From time to time he'll bring home an album by a group which, although they're talented, sing about some pretty questionable stuff. How much of a danger is there in this? Should we allow it to continue?

Answer: If you wanted to buy new carpet for your home and had the option of buying carpet made by a Christian firm or made by a non-Christian outlet, which carpet would you purchase? Some would select carpet made by the Christian. Personally, I'd buy the better rug. Likewise, if a child wants to learn to be the best at a particular instrument, he or she will greatly benefit from listening to the best player.

My first guitar lesson was in the sixth grade; Aunt Despe was gracious enough to teach me the basics which prompted me to seek professional classical guitar lessons a year later. Naturally, as a guitarist who played classical as well as folk and rock styles, I enjoyed listening to talented "guitar heroes" like Eric Clapton, Jimi Hendrix, Johnny Winter, and Alvin Lee. In my case, I had no difficulty separating their skill from their message. When I later learned of the incredibly talented Phil Keaggy, who also happened to be a Christian, I was thrilled! Here was a guy whom I could learn from while identifying with the heart of his songs. The best of both worlds!

In many instances, the superior musician will not be a Christian. Yet talent is talent. All talent comes from the Author of music. Your task will be to help that aspiring artist keep a sound perspective as he learns from the masters in their field. My advice would be to proceed with caution. Make this deal with your child: You will provide him with a lot of latitude in his study of popular musicians. But he will defer to your judgment and suspend his study if you notice negative attitude changes in him down the road.

To minimize any danger, be sure that you are spending plenty of time "nose to nose" with your youngster so you can identify the early stages of personality fluctuations. My folks gave me this kind of room to learn, while holding me accountable through the process.

9

LEAVING A LEGACY

We've traveled many miles in our analysis of the popular entertainment culture. We've taken a rather candid look at the media assault upon our families. And we've considered a number of suggestions to help us instill a discerning spirit in each of our family members. Like Rip Van Winkle, we've been asleep far too long, and we recognize something must be done. But is teaching our household the principles of "learn to discern" the end of our journey? Have we no further obligation to society? Should we be commending decency to our particular community? Is there a role that we ought to be playing in the national debate between those who believe in unrestricted freedom of speech versus those who desire to balance our freedoms with a commitment to social responsibility?

I've wrestled with these questions for the better part of my life. You see, a number of years ago, my staff and I were tired and close to burnout. It seemed every time we saw the signs of social responsibility emerge from the entertainment industries, another deviant product from Hollywood would flood the marketplace with its pollutants. Sitting around the meeting table one discouraging afternoon, I asked the staff: What are we trying to do, anyway? Wipe out *all* evil influences in America during our lifetime? How about 50 percent or 25 percent? Would we settle for a 10 percent reduction of immoral activity?

Scripture provided the answer. Jesus said, "You are the salt of the earth; but if the salt has become tasteless, how will it be made salty again? It is good for nothing anymore, except to be thrown out and trampled under foot by men. You are the light of the world" (Matthew 5:13–14). Our mandate while on earth is to "occupy" until the Lord returns. Since He's already won the battle, we're essentially in the "salt and light" business. What exactly does that mean? For one thing, God doesn't call us to be *successful;* He simply requires that we be *faithful* to season this dark world with the light of His Word. For another, it's clear that our "marching orders" compel us to leave the comfortable surroundings of home and church and enter the dialogue of the public square—to present biblical perspectives on proper individual and social conduct. Doing so provides the Lord with more avenues to multiply the impact of our legacy.

But marching orders can sound so cold and impersonal. Perhaps the following note from an inmate better underlines our need to be in the "salt and light" business.

> I am a prisoner in the Texas state system, convicted in 1984 of rape. I was quite guilty. I was raised in a good home, went to good schools, was normal in every way—even graduated from a Christian college. I was a successful free-lance and corporate media writer and producer. In 1980, however, I began to be attracted to pornography and the Dallas night scene. I frequented several strip joints and an "adult" bookstore. . . . in time I developed a fantasy about rape. I carried out that fantasy and will be sorry for it the rest of my life.
>
> I am grateful that I was stopped by the law, because I was out of control. I did not kill anyone and did not yet entertain such thoughts, but it is possible that that was the next step in my destructions. I would never have thought that I was capable of rape, either. That is my ugly story. I can never forgive myself for it and am determined to do what I can to make it right, although I realize that some things just cannot be undone.
>
> My main purpose in writing is to thank you for your efforts to prosecute the music of 2 Live Crew. I lowered myself to the standards of that group's message when I committed my crimes. I hope that you will never cease to enforce the law in such matters, because you are the last bastion between innocent victims and men such as I was, who actively will to lose control of themselves by partaking of destructive pornography or destructive music.
>
> This is not merely a "do good" letter by me or something to soothe my conscience. It is a call to arms for you, because if people can be hurt by me, they will be hurt by any man who fills himself with trash. Stop the trash, sir.

The inmate who wrote this letter originally addressed it to Sheriff Nick Navarro, the officer who thanklessly labored to apply Florida's obscenity laws to the lyrics of the rap group 2 Live Crew. Navarro's efforts ultimately led to a landmark legal determination by U.S. District Judge Jose Gonzalez on June 6, 1990, which determined *As Nasty As They Wanna Be,* by 2 Live Crew, to be legally obscene.

Although this young professional fueled his antisocial actions through more "traditional" forms of pornography—strip clubs, videos, and magazines—the million-selling album by 2 Live Crew is equally as degrading as its porno bookstore counterpart. Without a doubt, the audio pornography that has infiltrated the music teens enjoy sows the seeds of mind pollution and opens the doorway to further exploration for this generation of young people.

As more of us become actively enrolled in the salt and light business—every individual rebuilding the walls of decency in his local community—those in the "entertainment" industry who seek to profit from

---

"Without a doubt, the audio pornography that has infiltrated the music teens enjoy sows the seeds of mind pollution and opens the doorway to further exploration for this generation of young people."

---

the exploitation of our weaknesses would be shunned, not rewarded. More importantly, the subversion of the human spirit—and yes, the destructive behavior, whether personal or corporate, which a distressed soul produces—would affect a smaller portion of society. That is certainly one legacy well worth our efforts.

LIFE ON THE FRONT LINES

Let me provide you with a fair warning: the decision to be salt in a pluralistic, morally numb society often produces a bad taste in the mouths of the media makers who invariably take notice of your activity. Don't let that deter you. For when you are committed to do the right thing, the Lord will walk with you each step of the way. I could present a number of firsthand examples of the resistance you'll likely encounter, as well as the Lord's provision of strength when facing the opposition, but one illustration will suffice.

Frequently, I spend time browsing at the local record store to study the latest music releases. (It goes without saying that I am on the lookout for *both* positive and negative products.) One afternoon, late in the summer of 1989, I came across the then newly released double-album set by 2 Live Crew, *As Nasty As They Wanna Be*. I was already familiar with the lyrically abusive nature of this band, so I purchased a copy and gave it a listen to see what they were up to this time. Mind you, my record collection contains more than a thousand titles. So, for me to say that their album was the most degrading, hostile-to-women, pornographic recording that I've ever studied is not an overstatement.

Finding it hard to imagine that there would be a large audience for misogyny, I didn't immediately comment on *Nasty* in public. Instead, I watched the *Billboard* album chart for several weeks for signs of its popularity. Almost in disbelief, I noted a number of weeks later that *Nasty* sold more than one million copies. At that point I decided enough was enough. There was no way that I could stand on the sidelines while these pornographers molested the minds of young fans. Figuring most parents had no idea what record stores were selling to children—in many instances, regardless of their age—I worked with my small staff to transcribe the seventy-nine minutes of this audio pornography. The transcript filled twenty-eight single-spaced typed pages.

I then produced a lyrical analysis with this question in mind: "What would a child hear if he listened to this album only one time through?" As detailed previously, (see page 63 for a complete analysis) the disc contained some 226 uses of the "F" word and 87 references to oral sex.

Keep in mind, this is what one would hear listening to the record on the first pass. Other lyrical images included descriptions of male ejaculation (9), erections (6), group sex (4), rimming (oral/anal sex) (3), urination or feces (2), one mention of incest, and more than a dozen illustrations of violent sexual activity. Consider the implications of a youngster who listened to *Nasty* a mere *ten* times. This young person would be assaulted with 1,117 explicit descriptions of genitalia while hearing 870 encounters of oral sex.

Using the resources available to me—a radio commentary, a press release, and several articles presenting the issue—we spread the word.

Listening in Coral Gables, Florida, was attorney Jack Thompson. Armed with the facts, Thompson urged local law enforcement agents to prosecute 2 Live Crew in his community for their apparent violation of his state's obscenity statutes. His persistence ultimately led to Judge Jose Gonzalez's landmark decision which found *Nasty* legally obscene.

I watched with excitement as I witnessed individuals—just like you—make a difference in their communities. From Connecticut to South Carolina, Tennessee to Texas, parents, law enforcement agents, even teenagers, followed the lead and applied pressure on local retailers to suspend the sale of this hate-filled album. It's encouraging to know what one person can do.

LIVE—FROM NEW YORK

Not everyone who advocates greater social responsibility by members of the entertainment industry will be thrown to the "lion's den"—the den of biased news reporting. If, however, you find yourself in that situation, I can attest from personal experience, as you'll see in a moment, the Lord will be with you even there. Since my office was responsible for transcribing and analyzing 2 Live Crew's crude release, it was not a surprise when we were contacted by scores of national, regional, and local media.

What *did* present a curve were the back-to-back invitations to be on the "Geraldo" and "Phil Donahue" shows. Although I've been on a television set before, the prospects of sharing our findings before a national TV audience made my heart race. The producers of the "Donahue" program told me that they wanted a "balanced" panel to discuss the "hot" issue of explicit lyrics. I've since learned what they mean by the word *balanced*—five against two. Factoring in Phil's antagonistic style, we're talking more on the order of six against two!

Seated to my right were these "victims of censorship": Luther Campbell (lead singer of 2 Live Crew), Campbell's lawyer, Jello Biafra (responsible for the hard-core poster entitled "Penis Landscape" we discussed in chapter 4), Wendy O'Williams (former lead singer for the Plasmatics, who frequently appeared on stage with little more than electrical tape covering her nipples), and Mike Muir (lead singer of the band

Suicidal Tendencies). Family advocate Jack Thompson and I provided the "balance."

After twenty or so minutes of listening to the others moaning about censorship, racism, and other smoke screens typically employed to blur the real issue, I felt it was time to cut through their hypocrisy. How could they expect anyone to seriously evaluate the flood of obscenity in music without supplying the evidence in question? It was then that I *quoted one line* from the 2 Live Crew album under consideration—mind you, one tiny excerpt from this double-record set.

Why in the world would I quote those lyrics on national television? I did it primarily for the benefit of the "adults only" *studio* audience. Many times the direction of a program is shaped by the attitude of those in the studio. Since Donahue, along with the other panelists, were evading the evidence, there was no way those sitting on the set would fully understand the gravity of the problem we were discussing.

Let me also emphatically state that by no means was it my intention to expose children at home, who might have been watching, to even a brief sample of this rap group's depravity. That's why prior to the program I inquired about their use of a delay system. On three occasions I was assured that there would be an individual who would be "watching the program closely" for any objectionable language and would be able to catch it before it went over the air waves.

You Can't Say That on TV

It's funny what happens on *live* television when someone who should have been "bleeping" was sleeping. Whether he went on a break or simply wasn't paying attention, we'll never know. His error provided an opportunity for millions of viewers to actually hear for themselves what Donahue and company worked so hard to hide. Not everyone was pleased with what they heard. The studio phone lines lit up with complaints, and according to one news account, Phil's face turned "lobster red." As you can well imagine, the tone of the program changed dramatically.

Yet, what happened following my quotation of the 2 Live Crew lyrics amazes me to this very day. Phil asked *me* to apologize for quoting *their* lyrics. Interesting. Why didn't Phil ask 2 Live Crew to apologize to the 1.4 million families whose children are listening to their foul lyrics day after day? I did offer an apology. Thankfully, the Lord was in the middle of that hostile situation and provided me with the perfect retort: "We can sell this stuff to an eight-year-old, but we can't talk about it

---

"What happened following my quotation of the 2 Live Crew lyrics amazes me to this very day. Phil Donahue asked me to apologize for quoting their lyrics."

---

among adults—something is wrong." Even Phil's jaded audience could see through the hypocrisy and promptly applauded that response.

All the News That's Fit to Print

The following day I was contacted by CNN, "Crossfire," ABC, PBS, "The Larry King Show," *People, Time, Newsweek, New York Post,* and many, many other national and local media outlets. I spent more than nine hours on the phone discussing what happened on the "Donahue" show. Without exception, when I asked these reporters if he or she had read the lyrics or taken the time to read Judge Gonzalez's sixty-two-page decision that found *Nasty* obscene, or even listened to the album, not a single journalist had done his homework.

Not surprisingly, the *Washington Post* didn't. The *Fort Myers News Press* didn't. The *Miami Herald* didn't. Thirty-two news stories in *Billboard* magazine didn't. And the *Los Angeles Times* didn't either. When reporting on the debate over explicit lyrics found in 2 Live Crew's *Nasty* project, these "objective" news publications failed to reprint even one *example* of the problem.

Imagine that. Instead of providing the public with even one sample of explicit music, these journalists routinely applied their own labels, such as *censor* and *right-winged religious fundamentalist,* to the concerned parents and legislators who were working to protect young minds from hard-core, sexually deviant lyrics.

I had to laugh when I read news headlines like, "The debate over warning labels and explicit music heats up." What debate? The news media consistently fails to represent our side of the equation by refusing to print the explicit lyrics in question. When contacted by the *Los Angeles Times* for an interview on 2 Live Crew, I asked the reporter to kindly include *any* one verse from *any* one song found on *As Nasty As They Wanna Be* (recorded by 2 Live Crew). The lyrics on this million-selling album were so graphic, the reporter stated flatly, "Well, we can't print that stuff." I see. According to the aforementioned news publications there's no problem, but the lyrics are too obscene to reprint in a family newspaper.

Few reporters sided with us on this issue. One notable exception was syndicated columnist Mona Charen who observed: "When 2 Live Crew croons about busting open women's vaginas and watching them bleed, our opinion leaders fret about censorship but not what has become of us that we *enjoy* such 'entertainment.' . . . by calling something art, we elevate, purify, and even deify it, insisting that it needn't obey the usual standards of human morality. . . . Art has consequences. It is not coincidence that the society which reads *American Psycho* and listens to Guns N' Roses and laughs at Andrew Dice Clay is also the society in which 'date rape' is out of control on college campuses, children wear bulletproof vests to school, and one in ten teenage girls gets pregnant."[1]

I especially appreciated the perspective of John Leo, an essayist with *U.S. News and World Report.* He didn't hesitate to criticize fellow journalists for their "muffled" news coverage of explicit lyrics. Leo observed, "The marvel is that we somehow managed to conduct a national uproar over these low-life entertainers, while the press labored mightily to ensure that few of us knew what the low-lifes were actually saying. . . . Consider the de facto media blackout on the content of 2 Live Crew lyrics. A computer search of 108 American newspapers turned up only eleven mentions nationwide of the startling lyric that recommends tearing or damaging girls' vaginas."[2]

Regarding the media blackout of this evidence, my findings concur with Leo. Having read 192 different stories focusing on the 2 Live Crew debate, I found *a mere five articles* attempted to reprint even an edited version of the lyrics. Slightly more (twenty nine) printed the lyrical analysis that my office supplied. Instead of providing helpful information on this important subject, these writers hurled labels at me and my employer, Focus on the Family, calling us "zealous right-wingers," "a watchdog group on a pro-censorship quest," and accused us of being "concerned with controlling music and art."

On the contrary, until the media tells the public the truth by reprinting the evidence, it is they, not concerned parents and legislators, who are America's censors. We the public have been dealt a short hand by those who control the news agenda. Americans deserve to know the full story—the media censors continue to suppress it.

RESPONSIBLE SPEECH VERSUS A FREE-FOR-ALL

Putting the censorship smoke screen aside for a moment, does the First Amendment to the U.S. Constitution place any restrictions on speech? Are we allowed to use our speech to be as nasty, dishonest, or harmful as we wanna be? Can Hollywood create and market, in the name of free speech, *anything,* no matter how vile? The American Civil Liberties Union would have us believe so. And, not surprisingly, they argue that even the deplorable exploitation of children through child pornography should be protected by the Constitution (see figure 9.1).

"I INCLUDED THE WORDS TO 'AS NASTY AS THEY WANNA BE' BY 2 LIVE CREW TO PROVE THEY ARE NOT OBSCENE'. DID YOU GET ALL THAT MS. WILSON?"

Figure 9.1

It would be easy for you to become impatient at this point in our discussion. In a few paragraphs you might begin to wonder, "What's this have to do with me?" Actually, everything, especially if you make a decision to be salt and light in your community. Whether you decide to tackle hard-core porn at the local "family" video store, indecent television broadcasting, or the playing of explicit music on your children's school bus, there will be those who, like the ACLU, wrongly assert society cannot regulate these expressions. But the truth is, the law is on your side, and the few moments we take here can prepare you to leave a legacy of excellence, instead of decadence.

If the truth were known, many of us have been intimidated off of the front lines by the ACLU's misleading accusations; they would have us believe the Constitution guarantees *all* speech. Fearing to be branded an advocate of censorship, we keep our mouths closed while pornographers exploit the Constitution for their personal profits. But who's right? Are there limits to speech? If so, what are they?

The First Amendment states:

> Congress shall make no law respecting an establishment of religion, or prohibiting the free exercise thereof: or abridging the freedom of speech, or of the press: or the right of the people peaceably to assemble, and to petition the government for redress of grievances.

Point number one: The U.S. *Congress* is the focus of the parameters set forth in this provision. The First Amendment says nothing of what an individual state, local community, or the justice system may or may not do to curb speech that they deem harmful to the welfare of society. This should be of great encouragement to those who decide to take a stand for decency.

Point number two: Surprise! There are more than *fourteen* forms of speech not protected by the Constitution. My eyes were opened to that fact by Bill Kelly, a retired FBI special agent who dealt with obscenity cases. Until Bill explained these limits to speech, I had no idea that the law was, and continues to be, on our side. In the interest of space, I am not mentioning all of the cases that define limits to speech—such as perjury under oath, child pornography, sedition, or being in contempt of court—nor am I including a summary of all the decisions. I realize that you may desire to skim these legal cases, and that's okay for now. Yet I believe this material will one day be of great assistance to you as you enter the public square to debate the issue of responsible speech.

- *Limit 1: Libel, slander, defamation of character.* Chaplinsky v. New Hampshire (315 U.S. at 568: 1942) "Obscene, libelous, and insulting speech is not protected by the First Amendment. It is of such slight value that any benefit derived from it is clearly outweighed by the social interest of order and morality."
- *Limit 2: Speaking a prayer or giving religious instruction in public schools.* Engle v. Vitale (370 U.S. at 421: 1962)
- *Limit 3: Words that advocate illegal acts, including conspiracy or obstruction of justice.* Dennis v. United States (341 U.S. at 494: 1951)
- *Limit 4: Words that will lead to or threaten social harm.* Gitlow v. New York (268 U.S. at 652: 1925)
- *Limit 5: Words that create a "clear and present danger."* Schenk v. United States (249 U.S. at 47: 1919) Limits cited included yelling "fire" in a crowded theater. In his Opinion, Justice Holmes stated: "The right of expression is not absolute. Like other acts, expression is conditional and has boundaries set by the circumstances in which it is done."
- *Limit 6: A public address which interferes with the orderly movement of traffic.* Feiner v. New York (340 U.S. at 315: 1951) "When clear and present danger of riot, disorder, interference with traffic upon the public street or other immediate threat to public safety, peace or order appears, the power of the state to prevent or punish is obvious."
- *Limit 7: Copyright violations.* Zacchini v. Scripps Howard Broadcasting, Co. (1977) Although *ideas* are public domain, the *form* of expression those ideas take may be copyrightable. An individual is not permitted to violate another's copyright in the name of free speech.
- *Limit 8: Pretrial publicity that might interfere with a defendant's opportunity to secure a fair trial by his peers.* Chandler v. Florida (449 U.S. at 560: 1981)
- *Limit 9: False advertising.* Virginia Pharmacy Board v. Virginia Citizens Consumer Council (1976) This decision established the principle that advertising may be controlled when it is false, misleading, or takes undue advantage of its audience.

- *Limit 10: Obscenity.* Roth v. United States (354 U.S. at 476: 1957) Clearly established that obscenity is not protected speech and upheld a federal attempt to regulate obscene speech. It noted the "phrasing of the First Amendment was not intended to protect every utterance." Miller v. California (413 U.S. at 419: 1973) This decision tightened the definitional standards for obscenity and provided a three-part test to determine whether a work is legally obscene.

When considering the obscenity laws in relationship to the 2 Live Crew case, Judge Gonzalez emphatically stated, "To repeat, violation of the laws against obscenity is as much against the law as assault, rape, kidnapping, robbery, or any other form of behavior which the legislature has declared criminal. . . . To be redundant, obscenity is not a protected form of speech under the U.S. Constitution, with or without voluntary labeling. *It is a crime*" (emphasis his).[3]

You don't have to work at a big organization to apply these laws at the local level. In fact, there are a number of avenues readily available to you when you're ready to be salt and light to your community. For example, anyone can write a letter to the editor or pen a guest editorial for the newspaper. You can educate your chapter of the PTA, the school board, civic or church group. And don't underestimate the value of sharing your concern with retailers who stock and sell offensive videos, magazines, and recordings. A visit with the police chief to share your desire to see obscenity laws enforced in your town carries significant weight.

Thankfully, for the time being, the obscenity laws of the land are on our side.

SHARPENING MY ARROWS

Thousands of letters poured into my office in the wake of my appearances on the "Phil Donahue" and "Geraldo" programs. A few of those writing were misled by various accounts in the press which stated that I had lost my cool and swore at Donahue! (Keep in mind, I was quoting lyrics by 2 Live Crew.) Not always careful to verify the scoop, the Associated Press wire service spread this factually incorrect information, and newspapers around the country picked up and reprinted their inaccurate report. When confronted with what actually took place, the AP ran a correction, but by then, the damage was done. Several folks wrote and called for my resignation.

However, the overwhelming majority of those who contacted my office applauded our taking a stand against obscenity in music. Hundreds of parents pledged to do something in their homes and communities, now that they knew the truth. A number of teenagers wrote and asked what they might do in their areas to change the direction of the culture. And there were the encouraging letters from grandparents who offered consistent prayer support. But I'll never forget a letter by one mother who described her role in the cultural battle for the hearts and minds of the next generation.

> Dear Bob, I cannot thank you enough for your stand against the explicit and degrading music and films that Hollywood is selling to our children. As a mother of three little boys, I feel compelled to do something. Although I cannot join you on the front lines, I am working hard here in my home to "sharpen my arrows"—to prepare my children so that one day they will be ready to do their part for the Kingdom. I believe that the best contribution I can make is to ensure that when I release my "arrows," they will fly straight and true, hitting the mark with precision.

Her strategy for shaping a godly heritage in the home *and* in society is precisely on target.

LEAVING A LEGACY

In the few remaining pages, I'd like to zero in on the matter of creating a strong Christian family legacy. But as I do, let's not forget about our commitment to leave a positive legacy within our communities as well. Perhaps the letter we read at the beginning of this chapter from the prisoner in Texas will serve as a reminder of our obligation to society.

One of my all-time favorite Christian communicators is Chuck Swindoll. In his fantastic radio series entitled, "The Strong Family," Chuck posed a number of penetrating questions about creating a family legacy, questions that are especially germane to our present discussion. He asks, "What qualities and character traits are you passing down to your children? Are you actively involved in knowing your children, guiding them toward maturity? Or are you passively allowing their evil bents to run rampant?"[4]—evil bents that are fueled day in and day out by negativity in the media, I might add.

What can happen if we walk away from the task of guiding children around the land mines of their culture instead of directing them into the ways of mature thinking? As part of his study on strong families, Swindoll cited a rather revealing story of contrasts, one well worth passing along.

> The father of Jonathan Edwards was a minister and his mother was the daughter of a clergyman. Among their descendants were fourteen presidents of colleges, more than one hundred college professors, more than one hundred lawyers, thirty judges, sixty physicians, more than a hundred clergymen, missionaries and theology professors, and about sixty authors. There is scarcely any great American industry that has not had one of his family among its chief promoters. Such is the product of one American Christian family, reared under the most favorable conditions.
>
> The contrast is presented in the Jukes family, which could not be made to study and would not work, and is said to have cost the state of New York a million dollars. Their entire record is one of pauperism and crime, insanity and imbecility. Among their twelve hundred known descendants, three hundred ten were professional paupers, four hundred forty were physically wrecked by their own wickedness, sixty were habitual thieves, one hundred thirty were convicted criminals, fifty-five were victims of impurity, only twenty learned a trade (and ten of these learned it in a state prison), and this notorious family produced seven murderers.[5]

This story provides insight into the matter of time and our guidance. Do you desire to leave a godly legacy within your family and within society similar to that of the Edwards' inheritance? If so, the *time* we invest in our families today will move us closer to this exemplary model. George Gallup, Jr., places this challenge before us: "If more Americans could be persuaded to carve out of their three or four hours of television viewing each day a period of five minutes at bedtime and use this time to ask their child a simple question—'How did things go today?'—and *listen,* the result in terms of individual families and society as a whole could, I believe, be highly salutary."[6]

For those whose branch of the family tree is plagued with decay, let me underline something of critical importance: it doesn't matter how troublesome your personal background was. And, the issue isn't whether or not your folks taught you to be a critical thinker. The truth is, no

---

"Wherever you find yourself today, a new and dynamic family legacy is within reach, especially when you begin to teach the principles of discernment to those in your care."

---

matter how good or bad of a job your folks did raising you, the process of growing a sound family tree and becoming salt and light to your town can begin *today* with *you.*

Let me encourage you to do what the wisest king in all of history did. Faced with the enormous task of guiding the family of Israel, King Solomon prayed, "Give Thy servant an understanding heart to judge Thy people *to discern between good and evil"* (1 Kings 3:9a, emphasis added). Based upon my experience as one of five children in the De-Moss household, there's no doubt in my mind that your family can be guided to "love what the Lord loves and to hate what He hates." Wherever you find yourself today, a new and dynamic family legacy is within reach, especially when you begin to teach the principles of discernment to those in your care.

As my mother often reminds me, the journey of a thousand miles starts with the first step. May God richly bless you and your home, and grant courage as you set sail on this exciting adventure!

NOTES

Chapter 1: Asleep at the Wheel

1. "Dead Pets to a Human Sacrifice," *The Los Angeles Times*, 19 October 1988.
2. "Gang rape enrages New York," *USA TODAY*, 24 April 1989.
3. "12-year-old admits raping sister," *The Washington Times*, January 1990.
4. "Horror film incited murder," *AFA Journal*, July 1988.
5. "Slasher suspect found hanged," *USA TODAY*, 30 November 1988.
6. "Many kids say they'd like more gore on TV," *Star Tribune*, 6 November 1990.
7. "AMA Doc's Concerned about the Pulse of Popular Music," *Parental Guidance*, August 1990.
8. "1990 crime rate: Americans lead world in violence," *The Bradenton Herald*, 13 March 1991.
9. "A generation without morals?" *The Miami Herald*, 14 October 1990.
10. "Survey Documents Horror Film Impact on Youth Culture," press release by the National Coalition on Television Violence, 11 August 1989.
11. Taken from a letter to Michael Parkinson, 8 November 1991, by Mayor Tom Bradley on City of Los Angeles stationery.

Chapter 2: Madison Avenue: Selling Teens Short

1. Al Ries and Jack Trout, *Positioning: The Battle for Your Mind* (New York, NY: McGraw-Hill, 1981), 34.
2. "The Public Mind: Consuming Images," PBS VIDEO, New York, NY, 1989.
3. Chuck Swindoll, *The Strong Family* (Portland, OR: Multnomah Press, 1991), 118.
4. "The Public Mind: Consuming Images."
5. "Beyond the Ads . . . Obsession," *The Los Angeles Times*, 26 May 1991, *Calendar*, 5.
6. Ibid.

Chapter 3: Flirting with Delilah

1. "How the television culture has become our real religion," *Eternity*, November 1976.
2. The Motion Picture Association of America, *1989 U.S. Economic Review*, 9.
3. Ibid.

4. Although Webster's dictionary hasn't defined *vidiot* to date, I'd offer the following definition. *VIDIOT*—(noun) 1. An individual who spends more time viewing TV than participating in any other activity. 2. One who considers the *TV Guide* serious reading. 3. A person who can operate a remote control without looking at any of the buttons.

5. Kevin Perotta, *Taming the TV Habit* (Ann Arbor, MI: Servant Books, 1982), 70.

6. Ibid, 65.

7. "Children Having Children," *TIME*, 9 December 1985, 81.

8. *NFD Journal*, March 1986, 7.

9. "The Public Mind: The Illusion of News," PBS VIDEO, New York, NY, 1989.

10. "A Look Back at 30 Years of TV's 'Vast Wasteland'," *Los Angeles Times*, 9 May 1991.

11. "Is TV Sex Getting Bolder?" *TV Guide*, 8 August 1987, 2.

12. "TV Violence Still Common as Bush Signs TV Violence Act of 1990," National Coalition Against Television Violence, 21 January 1991.

13. "Redeeming the Time," *Jubilee*, February 1991.

14. "Renouncing TV for Lent," *The Philadelphia Inquirer*, 8 March 1987.

Chapter 4: The Decade the Music Died

1. Dr. David Elkind, *The Hurried Child* (Redding, MA: Addison Wesley Publishing Company, 1988), 89–93.

2. "Dead Liberties," *Playboy*, October 1986.

3. "Table Manners," *LA WEEKLY*, 16–22 August 1991.

4. "Guns N' Roses," *Rip*, February 1990.

5. "Today They're Trying to Censor Rap, Tomorrow. . . ," *The Los Angeles Times*, 5 November 1990.

6. Press release by the NAACP, June 1990.

7. Ibid.

8. "Personalities," *The Washington Post*, 29 November 1990.

9. "MTV Pulls Madonna's Latest Video—For Now," *Parental Guidance*, January 1991.

10. ABC's "Nightline."

11. "Brutal Rap Lyrics," "Good Morning America" transcript, 9 July 1991.

12. "Low 'Priority': N.W.A's Chart-Topping Album," *Billboard*, 6 July 1991.

13. "Too-slick rappers sell rage, despair for profit," *The Miami Herald*, 27 July 1991.

14. "A Nasty Jolt for the Top Pops," *Time*, 1 July 1991.

15. Ibid.

16. "N.W.A's Latest Ghetto Blast Takes Off in Middle America," *The Los Angeles Times*, 15 June 1991.

17. "Rap song linked to gang rape," *The Tulsa Tribune*, 8 June 1990.

18. "Experts Debate Influence of Violent Music on Youths," *The Los Angeles Times*, 19 October 1988.

Chapter 5: Setting the Standard

1. "The Teen Environment—A Study of Growth Strategies," The Robert Johnston Company, 1986.

2. "The Rebirth of America," (Philadelphia, PA: Arthur S. DeMoss Foundation, 1986), 37.

3. Kenneth A. Myers, *All God's Children and Blue Suede Shoes* (West Chester, IL: Crossway Books, 1989), xiii.

4. "News elite feel they should have most power," Reprinted by the *NFD Journal*, October 1986, 11–13.

5. Ibid.

6. "Pornography and our children." Taken from a speech by Gary L. Bauer at the Morality in Media National Convention, Orlando, FL, 30 October 1987.

Chapter 6: Getting a Grip

1. Dana Key with Steve Rabey, *Don't Stop the Music* (Grand Rapids, MI: Zondervan Publishing House, 1989), 149–150.

2. Ibid., 150.

Chapter 7: Dancing to the Beat of a Different Drummer

1. Dr. and Mrs. Cannon, "Striving for Excellence—How to Evaluate Music" (Oak Brook, IL: The Institute in Basic Life Principles, 1989). As much as I respect the fine work to strengthen the home by Mr. Bill Gothard and the Institute, their approach to music in this and other publications is simply poor scholarship. I will continue to applaud their family seminar series, but will, for now, find their evaluation of music unacceptable.

2. Dana Key with Steve Rabey, *Don't Stop the Music* (Grand Rapids, MI: Zondervan Publishing House, 1989), 70–71.

3. Ibid., 71.

4. Portions reprinted with permission from "Help Your Children Change Their 'Tunes'" by Bob DeMoss, Focus on the Family's *Parental Guidance*, November 1990.

Chapter 9: Leaving a Legacy

1. "When are you decadent?" Mona Charen, copyrighted by the Creators Syndicate, Inc., 1990.

2. "Ugly truths untold by the press," John Leo, *U.S. News and World Report*, 10 September 1990, 23.

3. Excerpt taken from the *Final Order* of Skywalker Records, Inc.; Luther Campbell; Mark Ross; David Hobbs; and Chris Wongwon; Plaintiffs, vs. Nicholas Navarro, Defendant. 6 June 1990, 13.

4. "The Strong Family" study guide, Insight for Living, 43.

5. As quoted by J. Oswald Sanders in *A Spiritual Clinic* (Chicago, IL: Moody Press, 1958), 90.

6. George Gallup, Jr., Testimony before the U.S. Senate Subcommittte on Family and Human Services, 22 March 1983.

SUBJECT INDEX

ABOUT THE AUTHOR

*F*or more than ten years, Robert DeMoss, Jr., has been committed to teaching the skills of discernment to parents and young people alike. In his role as youth culture specialist for Focus on the Family, DeMoss uses seminar presentations to equip parents, church and civic leaders, educators, and young people with the tools to make sound entertainment choices. DeMoss' educational efforts have been noted and applauded by *TV Guide,* Ann Landers, *Reader's Digest,* and the White House Conference for a Drug-Free America.

In addition to his speaking schedule, DeMoss pens a monthly column in two teen magazines, *Breakaway* and *Brio,* for Focus on the Family. He is the editor of *Parental Guidance,* a monthly newsletter for parents on popular youth culture. A former disc jockey and musician, DeMoss has debated the issue of explicit lyrics on national television, including appearances on the "Phil Donahue" show, "Geraldo," and "Good Morning America." He resides in Colorado Springs, Colorado.

NOW ON VIDEO
LEARN TO DISCERN

*E*very day, the media feeds our youth a steady diet of unhealthy images—violence, sex, suicide, and the occult—that manipulate their minds, and exploit their fears. Even more frightening, children often embrace the activities they see glamorized. Find out what you can do to prepare your children to combat these harmful messages.

Now in Focus on the Family Films' new video, Robert DeMoss Jr., Focus's Youth Culture Specialist, offers hope to parents, educators and youth leaders by providing positive solutions to the media's fixation with violence and other socially adverse behaviors. After viewing "Learn to Discern: Help for a Generation at Risk" you will be equipped to teach adolescents how to think critically and "Christianly" about the voices of the popular entertainment culture—music, film, advertising and television.

See your local Christian Bookstore or write to Focus on the Family, Colorado Springs, CO 80995.